God Did It, But How?

Second Edition

Robert B. Fischer, Ph.D.

ASA Press
American Scientific Affiliation
55 Market St., P.O. Box 668
Ipswich, MA 01938-0668

Contents

Preface

The subject matter of this book deals with the relationships between the Bible and science. This has been an area of considerable popular concern for many years, particularly as it involves the origins of life and human beings. Much of what is written and taught within evangelical Christian circles takes one particular viewpoint, while what is written and taught in some liberal circles (and also assumed in virtually all other non-evangelical circles) takes another viewpoint. The former is so unacceptable scientifically and the latter so unacceptable biblically that the controversy turns into emotional outbursts and senseless ridicule emanating from both sides. The practical consequences indeed are serious.

As one whose vocation for many years has been that of an academic scientist in research, teaching, and administration and whose avocation has long been biblical studies and hermeneutics, I am deeply troubled by this state of affairs. I feel that I understand and respect both viewpoints but find serious misunderstanding and error in both. I am convinced that there is a more basic viewpoint which is thoroughly biblical and scientifically sound. I claim no originality in concept — much of it is often discussed and described by scientists and other scholars who are dedicated Christians. However, I sense a continuing need for a clear written presentation for consideration by average people, including those who are evangelical Christians and all persons who have even modest respect for science. This book is an attempt to contribute toward meeting that need.

I attempt to be positive throughout, not to tear down or to criticize others, but rather to present positively what I consider to be the valid viewpoint in this area. Whether or not readers in general can agree that this is the one valid viewpoint, I surely think that it should be available as an alternative to the polarized ones which currently are available to the lay reader.

The preceding three paragraphs are taken from the earlier edition of this book. The purpose and general thrust remain unchanged for this second edition. Several sections have been rewritten, especially in chapters one and three, and numerous changes have been made throughout. All of these changes have been made for one or both of two reasons: to clarify statements that were found to be either unclear or unduly subject to misinterpretation, and to insure that the content is reasonably up-to-date at this time. In addition, a list of suggested supplemental readings is included, in response to suggestions from a number of readers of the earlier edition.

I am deeply appreciative of all those who have shared their comments with me after reading the earlier edition of the book. Many have commented favorably, including a few who totally disagree with the general thrust. Others have been very harsh and negative in their criticisms, including some who have talked or written about me to others but not to me. In sum, however, all of the comments have been considered and have been beneficial.

I am especially appreciative of the following persons, each of whom has read, or reread, the earlier edition carefully with the specific intent of making suggestions for this revision: Richard H. Bube, Edward B. Davis, John W. Haas, Jr., John L. Wiester, and David L. Wilcox. Thanks are due also to Donald W. Munro, John W. Haas, Jr., Lyn Berg, Carol Aiken, and their colleagues in the leadership of the American Scientific Affiliation, for their efforts in initiating and facilitating this project. Special thanks to my wife, Mary Ellen, for checking over the manuscript. Comments from readers are invited.

Robert B. Fischer

Chapter One
Who, What, How and Why?

What are the relationships between science and the Bible? Is knowledge obtained by scientific investigation of nature compatible with knowledge obtained by study of the Bible? What about intellectual activity and faith — do they reinforce each other, or are they contradictory, or are they independent of each other? Is there any reality other than the realm of nature, or is even that illusory, and how can we find out? Is there such a "thing" as the supernatural and, if so, how does it relate, if at all, to the natural? How does God enter into all of these considerations? How do human beings? Can a person be a "good" scientist and a Bible-believing Christian? What about creation and evolution — must I choose one or the other, or may I hold to both, or reject both, or are they even alternatives to each other? How do these considerations relate to me as an individual, or I to them?

These questions are of considerable contemporary interest to many people, Christians and non-Christians alike, and such has been the case for years and generations past. These questions involve areas of knowledge and understanding in which there are now and long have been controversies, problems, confusions, and differences of understanding.

Much of the controversy, I think, arises from inadequate, inaccurate, and distorted understandings of the essence and content of scientific and intellectual activity and also of biblical study. The inevitable results of these distortions are in evidence, in that controversies remain unresolved with people needlessly polarized one from another, and with too much attention diverted by pseudo-issues from the real issues and problems which do exist.

It is not my expectation that this book will resolve these issues. Laudable as such a goal might be, it would surely be very unrealistic to expect any finality in reaching it. Rather, it is the intent in this book to center attention on certain aspects of the overall issues, with the hope that some of us who disagree with each other in our understandings may at least have a better meeting of the minds about what it is that we disagree about. Perhaps in so doing we may even clarify some of our own thinking and understandings.

In this chapter, we will analyze the title of the book by considering briefly four words which are directly or indirectly involved — who, what, how, and why? We will also identify sources of information to which we may turn as we seek answers to these questions.

Who?

The "who" with which we are concerned here is stated in the title to be God. By this we mean the God who exists and who is the God of the Bible. Many theological statements have been formulated to identify and to give specificity to the biblical concept of God. One of the most comprehensive of these is that of the Westminster Shorter Catechism, "God is a spirit, infinite, eternal, unchangeable, in his being, wisdom, power, holiness, justice, goodness and truth." Perhaps the meaning of this statement may be clarified by writing it as a diagram.

God is a spirit,	infinite eternal unchangeable	in his	being, wisdom, power, holiness, justice, goodness and truth.

This is the God who is both transcendent and immanent. By transcendent, we mean that God extends beyond the material universe, that God is infinite and thus is not limited to the finite characteristics of the universe of matter and energy. By immanent, we mean that God is within the material universe, that he somehow indwells it, and is not solely remote from it or isolated from it. To illustrate the significance of these terms, consider two alternative views of God: deism and pantheism. Deism recognizes transcendence but not immanence. In this view, God created the universe and left it to run by itself, as a watchmaker makes a watch, winds it up, and then lets it run. Pantheism recognizes a form of immanence but not transcendence. God is identified with all that is. In this view, all finite things are parts of, or appearances of, some ultimate being which may be designated as God. God is neither apart from nature nor found within nature. Nature is God and God is nature. It is the unique combination of the transcendence and immanence of God that distinguishes the biblical view of God from deism and pantheism and other concepts of God.

Both the transcendence and the immanence of God are referred to in a discourse on the being and nature of God by the Apostle Paul in Acts 17:22-34. The transcendence underlies statements that God is not made of matter: "since He is Lord of heaven and earth, does not dwell in temples made with hands" (verse 24), and "we ought not to think that the Divine Nature is like gold or silver or stone, an image formed by the art and thought of man" (verse 29), and the statement that he is the Creator of humankind: "and He made from one blood every nation of mankind to live on all the face of the earth" (verse 26). The immanence of God is involved in the statements that he is currently the Sustainer and the Overseer of all life including human beings: "He Himself gives to all life and breath and all things" (verse 25), "for in Him we live and move and exist" (verse 28), and "though He is not far from each one of us" (verse 27).

We are not attempting here to discuss in detail evidences for the existence or the nature of God. We are simply identifying the God of the Bible as the one whose doings are the subject matter of this book.

What?

Our title states, "God did it." So, what is the "it?" By "it" we mean whatever God does. More specifically, however, we will concern ourselves in this and subsequent chapters with several things which God has done or now does in the realm of nature. By nature, we mean the realm of matter and energy, of space and time, and the fundamental laws which describe the actions and reactions which take place therein.

It is in the realm of nature that all of us exist as human beings. This is the realm with which we are in contact by means of our senses, and in which we have experiences. It is the realm in which human beings can study and gain knowledge through scientific methods of investigation, and which is described by means of scientific knowledge.

Biblical knowledge and scientific knowledge may at times overlap to the extent that both deal with the same natural objects and phenomena. To be sure, the Bible is not predominantly a source book of scientific knowledge; and a treatise on modern science in the area of chemistry, biology, or geology is not predominantly a source book of biblical knowledge. But to the extent that both deal with natural phenomena and with events and materials which exist in the realm of nature, it is possible that the knowledge which one contains may either overlap or supplement the other. Several instances of this type of overlap, or at least of perceived overlap, are considered the "it" and the "what" in this book.

How?

It is not always possible to separate totally the "who" from the "how." Yet it is important that we try to do so to the extent that they are separable, and to recognize clearly the overlap that exists when an answer to one necessarily implies a particular answer to the other.

In describing phenomena in the realm of nature, the answer to a how question normally consists of a statement of cause-and-effect relationships within nature. It consists of an identification of the natural means and mechanisms which preceded or accompanied the phenomenon of interest and thus were involved in causing it.

Consider, as examples, such questions as how a tree leaf changes color in the fall, how a plant grows, how electrical energy is produced in a battery, how chlorine gas reacts with water molecules, how an aspirin tablet works in relieving headache symptoms, or how an airplane stays up in the air. Each answer consists of an explanation within the realm of nature, dealing with matter and energy and the physical/chemical/biological laws which describe natural actions and reactions. A detailed answer to the question of how may be given without considering anything about the who question; the latter may even be inconsequential to the former.

Next, consider questions which deal with single events rather than with repetitive events, as did those in the preceding paragraph. Consider, for example, how the pyramids in Egypt were built, how Columbus crossed the ocean, how this person or that one caught a cold, or how the car fender became dented. For these questions, too, the answers consist of statements from the realm of nature describing the natural means and mechanisms by which these developments occurred. Also, as before, the how questions may be answered independently of considering who did it. However, it may or may not be possible to separate the questions of how it was done and who did it.

Any of these sample how questions could be changed into a who question. For example, who causes a tree leaf to change color in the fall, who causes the chlorine and water molecules to react with each other, who built the pyramids in Egypt, or who caused this person or that one to catch cold? Whether each of these appears to be a particularly meaningful question or not, one point is clear: the who question is distinctly different from the how question.

One conceivable answer to the question, "Who causes a tree leaf to change color in the fall?" is that God does it. This means that it is done by the God of the Bible, who is transcendent to nature and who is acting in this way as immanent in nature. For one to answer the who question in this way does nothing whatever to anticipate any particular answer to the question of how the leaf changes color. Indeed, even if one answers the who question by declaring that God does it, there is surely nothing out-of-place or sacrilegious for one to proceed to the how question with full expectation of arriving at an explanation consisting entirely of natural cause-and-effect relationships and mechanisms. Similarly, we could first answer the how question correctly and entirely from within the realm of nature, without in any way anticipating any particular answer to the who question. In fact, a person, who sincerely believes the correct answer to the who question is that God does it, and another person, who is sincerely atheistic or agnostic, may both answer the how question correctly in the same way.

This distinction between the questions, who and how, may seem to be too elementary and obvious. Yet it is my view that much of the conflict and the confusing differences of understanding, which have long engulfed considerations of the relationship between the Bible on the one hand, and science and intellectual activity on the other hand, arise directly from a blurring together of the distinctive differences between who questions and how questions dealing with topics in nature on which the two sources of information overlap.

Why?

Our title does not contain the word "why," nor is it even implied in any very direct way. However, it is related to the questions of who and how in dealing with various things that God does or has done in the realm of nature. So, a few brief comments on why questions may be in order.

There are at least two different ways in which the word why is used in our everyday conversation and thinking. One is in reference to the immediate cause which precedes, and results in, the effect which is of interest. The answer to such a question as this is really a statement of the natural means or mechanism involved, and the why question is essentially the same as a how question. For example, why does iron rust, or why does body temperature go up when one is ill, or why does a transistor radio use less electrical power than a tube type radio, or why does the sky sometimes appear red at sunset? The answers to these why questions may properly consist of statements of physical or chemical laws or cause-and-effect relationships within the realm of nature.

Another common usage of the word why is concerning the intent or purpose of the one who did it. When used in this sense, a why question is closely related to a who question. For example, why did you buy a new car, or why are so many reruns shown on summer television, or why does the American League use the designated hitter rule while the National League does not, or why do you try to teach good manners to your children, or why does one engage in jogging or other regular exercise? The answers to all these questions consist of statements of the intent or purpose of the people who cause the actions to occur or the situations to exist. The purpose may be deliberate, or it may be present without being realized, or it may even be coincidental.

Many why questions may not appear to fit neatly into either of these two categories, but they generally do revolve around considerations of how or who or both. Furthermore, the significance of anything is really determined largely by some combination of what it is, how it is done or has come into being, who did it, and the purpose for which it was done.

Sources of Information

Since we are to consider in this book the identification of some things which God has done that involve the realm of

7

nature and how God did them, it is important for us to state clearly at the outset what our sources of information are. Whether you agree that the use of each of these sources is valid or not, we should at least have a common understanding of the basis on which we are proceeding.

There are two sources from which we will obtain the information that we will use and accept in the chapters which follow. One is the Bible; the other is the scientific investigation of nature. However, simply to state this is insufficient. Additional comment and explanation are essential, if we are even to approach a common understanding of what is meant by this straightforward statement of what our two sources of information are.

The processes of gaining knowledge from these two sources are very similar in some significant respects and different in others. In each process, there is (a) input, which consists essentially of "what is there" in the Bible or in the realm of nature, but this is only the beginning of the process. The observational input leads to (b) interpretation and other processing of that input by appropriate methodology, which leads to (c) output, commonly designated as biblical or theological explanation or as scientific explanation. The output leads to (d) prediction of further observational tests and test results to prove or to negate that explanation and thus to a repetition of the cycle. There is a logical progression of the four steps in the order indicated. However, the steps may overlap, and all may be concurrent in the sense that one need not be completed before the next one begins.

The methodologies used in step (b) with the two sources of information are essentially similar in principle but different in some practical ways because of the different sources of input. The term "rational inquiry" is applicable to both. Indeed, the overall processes of gaining information from the Bible and from the scientific investigation of nature are so similar that it was fashionable in an earlier era to refer to theology as the queen of the sciences — "sciences" because of the methodology and "queen" because its subject matter deals with a transcendent God.

Let us now identify some distinctive aspects of gaining information from each of the two sources.

Information from the Bible

We are taking the Bible, consisting of the Old and New Testaments, to be the written Word of God and thus to be reliable and authoritative. Strictly speaking, this statement applies to the original writings of the various books and not to any particular modern translation or paraphrase. To be sure, we do not now have access to any of the original manuscripts, but we do have the results of careful study and analysis of literally thousands of ancient manuscripts and portions of manuscripts. There is accordingly little or no uncertainty about the conclusion that modern translations do indeed provide generally reliable information about the content of the originals. So the concept that the Bible is reliable and authoritative is generally applicable to these modern translations.

The books which are generally accepted as comprising the Bible are commonly designated as canonical books and the complete list as the canon of the Bible. These particular books were not the only ones written on similar subjects around the same time, and probably even by some of the same human authors. So why are these books included and not others?

There have been some disagreements over the years about which ones should be included as canonical books. For example, the Roman Catholic and Protestant Bibles differ by the inclusion or exclusion of the so-called "apocryphal" books. Indeed, this issue was debated intensively for many centuries, even before the time of the Protestant Reformation. As an example of a different type, the Old Testament of Judaism includes several instances in which a single book consists of a combination of two or more of the books in the Protestant Old Testament, and the order in which the books are listed is somewhat different. Nevertheless, the content is the same in the Old Testaments of Judaism, Protestantism, and, apart from the apocryphal books, Roman Catholicism.

It is beyond the scope of this book to review in detail the historical record of how these particular books were chosen to comprise the Bible, fascinating as this topic is. Suffice it to state here that we are accepting as valid the common canons of the Old and New Testaments, as they now exist. The variations which are now found in these listings, both in arrangement and in actual content, are relatively minor and do not in any significant way have bearing on the use of the Bible for our present purposes.

The statement that we are accepting the Bible as reliable and authoritative is by no means a simple one. The Bible consists of words, and words are really nothing more or less than symbols which represent concepts, ideas, and objects. The real meaning is in those concepts, ideas, and objects and not in the symbols which represent them. Therefore, it is essential and inevitable that the words be interpreted in order for one to understand their meaning.

To claim that one can simply read and understand the Bible — or any other written document for that matter — without interpretation is not valid. To claim that the Bible interprets itself, as is often done, may be valid at least in part. However, even that does not negate the essential role of interpretation, for the meaning and the reality are in the interpretation, not merely in the words which are interpreted.

The principles and procedures of biblical interpretation comprise a very fascinating field of investigation and study and of active research and development, but this too is beyond the scope of this book. However, we will necessarily be engaged in the practice of interpretation, so a brief summary of the process and the principles of interpretation which we are accepting and using is of interest here.

There are three basic principles of interpretation: language, context, and history and culture. Under the heading of language, we must be concerned with several types of consideration, such as the following:

(a) the identification of what the words are, ultimately what they were in their original languages
(b) which of several alternative meanings is really intended (for example, does the English word "church" refer to a building, an activity, a local group, or a larger group?)
(c) the general and specific characteristics of the language (for example, the Greek language is highly agglutinative, which means that very fine shades of meaning are denoted by the choice of which one of many forms of the same word is used)
(d) with technical meanings of words as compared to their common meanings (for example, the modern English word "element" has a technical meaning in chemistry which is quite different than in its use by people talking about the weather, or the word "inspiration" has a technical meaning in biblical studies which is quite different than its use by people describing their reactions to an orchestral rendition of Tchaikovsky's *1812 Overture*).

Because of these and other factors, the translation of anything from one language to another is not simply a process of word-by-word replacement. Furthermore, every language changes to some extent over time. This is one reason why a modern English translation of the Bible may be more accurate in communicating its content to today's readers than is an English translation prepared several centuries ago.

Under the heading of context as a principle of interpretation, we include such considerations as the immediate context in which a word or sentence occurs, the nature of the book in which it is written (for example, is the book primarily historical, pastoral, poetic, or prophetic), parallel accounts which may supplement each other (for example, some parallel or overlapping accounts are found in Kings and Chronicles, in historical and prophetic Old Testament books, in the four gospels, and in Acts and some New Testament epistles), the principle of progressive revelation (for example, God revealed his law in the Ten Commandments, and then later added Jesus' interpretation of it in the Sermon on the Mount).

Under the heading of history and culture, we recognize (a) that the books of the Bible were initially written to people in historical and cultural settings different from our own, and (b) that it claims to have information applicable and significant for people in various historical and cultural settings including our own and others as well. In a sense, we can consider the history and culture to form a part of the context which is important in interpretation. However, we have other sources of information about many of the historical incidents and conditions described in the Bible, the geographical locations where they occurred, and the societal factors which were involved. These additional sources of information can be helpful in interpretation.

Biblical authors used various figures of speech from time to time, as do many contemporary writers and speakers. Similes, metaphors, personifications, understatements and overstatements, and parables are found in the Bible. Each figure of speech, if it is to be interpreted properly, must be identified as to what it is. Generally this is made possible by application of the same principles which have already been listed. Prophecy occupies an important place in the writings of the Bible. Its proper interpretation requires particular emphasis on the nature of prophecy in general as it is used in the Bible. This is an area in which there is even now considerable misunderstanding and difference of understanding.

Biblical interpretation is a field of research for scholarly experts, but it is also an area of activity in which lay people can become deeply and meaningfully involved. This situation is analogous to the interpretation of the plays of Shakespeare — these writings, too, can be read and interpreted by experts engaged in scholarly research on them, and also by the rest of us for our own enjoyment, edification, and interest.

The principles and processes of interpreting the Bible are really very similar to those of interpreting other written and oral usages of words, whether it be in the area of literature, scholarly works in any field of study, historical works, legal documents, or even current newspapers and everyday conversation. Furthermore, there is no need for one to agree that the Bible is God's Word in order to engage in interpreting it. A "believer" and a "nonbeliever" may interpret a particular part of the Bible in the same way, except for their differences of understanding who is its "ultimate author."

Another factor in the interpretation of the Bible, which is unique and very important, is the role of the Holy Spirit in enabling a believer to understand what is contained within the Bible. A careful study of this topic in 1 Corinthians 2:10-14 and related biblical passages reveals that

  (a) the Holy Spirit indwells the believer ("we have received the Spirit who is from God"),
  (b) the Holy Spirit enables these people to understand and to accept that which has been revealed to humankind by God ("that we may know the things freely given to us by God"), and
  (c) to the nonbeliever ("natural man") some things are "foolishness to Him and He cannot understand them."

A specific example is given in 1 Corinthians 1:23-24, where the preaching of the crucified Christ is identified as "foolishness" to the nonbeliever and as the "power of God" to the believer. Thus, the Holy Spirit indwelling the believer, while not providing any additional information, enables the believer to understand and appreciate more of the real significance of that which God has revealed in the Bible. Both the believer and the nonbeliever can read the same things in the Bible, even with the same definitions in mind about what those words mean. However, they differ markedly in their understanding and acceptance of the deeper import of what the words and statements signify, ranging from "foolishness" to "the power of God."

An additional comment of the authoritativeness of the Bible is in order. We are taking the Bible to be authoritative, and we stated that interpretation is both necessary and inevitable. These two factors may appear to be inconsistent. Yet they do fit together. It is the Bible itself, and not any particular interpretation of it that is authoritative. Interpretations are to be verified and challenged by appealing to the Bible itself and by re-examination of the interpretation. This does not mean that interpretations are to be challenged and discarded at will or because of personal preference, but it does mean that an interpretation is valid only to the extent that it correctly represents the Bible.

Information from the Study of Nature

Besides the Bible, we are taking the scientific investigation of nature as a valid source of information about what God has done which involves the realm of nature. This type of investigation, of course, leads to knowledge of nature, matter and energy, and the laws which describe their actions and interrelationships. However, it does not necessarily prove unequivocally that God is the "doer." Nevertheless, it may provide substantiating evidence for one who by faith believes that God is the primary cause underlying all of nature. The same evidence, however, may not be at all convincing for one who does not have that faith or who has a conflicting faith.

The practice of science is a human activity, and the general methodology by which it is done is commonly referred to as the scientific method. From much of what has been written in popular sources about the scientific method of gaining, establishing, and refining knowledge, it would almost seem as if this method is like an efficient machine or recipe, by which, if one follows a set procedure, the desired results are forthcoming. This concept is an oversimplification at best, very misleading at worst, and fails to describe what the practice of science really is.

As noted above, the essential ingredients in scientific methodology are (a) observation in the realm of nature, which leads to (b) interpretation and correlation of that which is observed, which leads to (c) scientific explanation, which leads to (d) prediction of further observational tests to substantiate or to negate that explanation. The methodology throughout must be, of course, appropriate for this type of input, which differs markedly from that found in biblical and theological study. So let us note some features of the scientific method.

In making observations, the worker in science may use his or her unaided natural senses of sense, sound, smell, touch, and taste, and also may use instruments and devices of many different types to aid the senses. The powers of sight may be extended to distant objects by means of telescopes, to minute objects and fine detail on larger objects by means of microscopes, to quantitative measures of color and intensity of light by photoelectric cells and spectrometers, and to recordings for future comparisons by photographic film or by electronic means. Many other sorts of electrical and mechanical phenomena can be converted by means of instruments to meter readings, computer printouts, tape recordings, and so forth into forms in which the observer can sense them.

As human beings engage in the practice of science and come to some particular facets of the realm of nature to make observations, they do so with all of their powers of observation, calling on all of the observational skills and tools available to them. In addition, they do so with some combination of presuppositions and mindsets, and with some "theory" to be tested. Some of these presuppositions and mindsets may be very specific and may have been developed consciously; some may be very vague and may even be outside a person's own awareness. Some may be believed with a considerable degree of confidence, and some may be considered to be possible but not likely. The "theory" to be tested may be quite specific and refined, or it may be nothing more than a mere hunch, guess, or expression of curiosity. It may have arisen from any source.

A scientist, never content with a single observation, insists on repeated observation of whatever phenomena are under investigation and reports the results so clearly that other people may repeat the observations and, hopefully, verify the results. The observations most frequently include quantitative measurements of some sort, since a quantitative or even semiquantitative result of an observation is more directly subject to being repeated, verified, and interpreted than is one which is strictly descriptive.

Observation requires interpretation if it is to be meaningful. The selection of a suitable basis or framework for the correlation is a human process, although it obviously must be appropriate somehow for the particular situation. This selection frequently must be made ahead of time to insure that appropriate data are obtained. Even so, it may be altered as the cyclic process of observation and interpretation continues.

Scientific explanation generally consists of statements of cause-and-effect relationships within the realm of nature. These statements are in words and/or numbers and other mathematical symbols. This means, of course, that the scientific explanation itself requires interpretation by anyone who would understand it.

A theory or theoretical explanation of phenomena which are observed is often assumed to be derived by purely inductive processes from the observations. This concept bears a measure of validity, but it is an oversimplification that overlooks the very significant role of creativity and imagination in scientific work. It is evident that there is not necessarily any logical bridge from phenomena to theoretical explanations of them, as has been pointed out by Einstein and others. In proposing a theoretical explanation, a scientist is guided by complex combinations of presuppositions, prior understandings and biases, as well as observations and experimental data. It is also always conceivably possible that more than one theoretical explanation can be placed on a given set of data. The scientist must always be alert to alternative possibilities.

Some proffered scientific explanations are called "models." A scientific model is a theoretical scheme, which may be anything from a mere guess to one that has been substantiated to a high level of confidence, but which in either case is still subject to further testing and modifications. Also, models are things selected to describe similarity between the model and the reality in certain respects, though there may be very major differences in other features. For example, our awareness of the solar system was formerly used, and occasionally still is used, as a model to describe the structure of an atom. There are similarities, but only in a very limited sense.

Scientific methodology does not stop with the formulation of a scientific explanation. Rather, the proffered explanation is used to predict further observational results, which are then tested by more experimentation and observations. The results of testing the predictions may lend either positive or negative support to the generalized concept and explanation. If the test corroborates the prediction, the postulated theory warrants a higher level of confidence and acceptance. If it is contradicted, the theory is more likely in need of modification or rejection. If neither corroborated nor contradicted, the test has not been fruitful with respect to this situation. Frequently, the test result does not clearly corroborate or contradict the prediction but falls somewhere in between — herein lies much of the challenge and excitement of scientific work.

For prediction and further testing to be possible, the generalized explanation must be formulated so that it is testable. A theory which does not lead to further experimentation, and thus either to further substantiation or to negation, is simply not useful in the practice of science. However, whether or not it is scientifically useful does not necessarily have any bearing on whether or not it is true.

It is important to note that a positive confirmation does not really prove that the proffered explanation is correct, only that it may be correct. It is always conceivable that some subsequent tests may negate the validity of the generalization and/or that some alternative explanation could be made of the same test results.

This leads us to the question about the truth of any scientific explanation, about whether we can ever really know that any scientific explanation is true. Truth is one of many words which are used frequently in everyday thinking and communication that have meaning but are hard to define. Somehow, a principle which is true has rightness rather than wrongness. Somehow, one truth is consistent with other truths rather than contradictory to them. Somehow, that which is true is not false; it is correct and not erroneous. Basically, that which is true corresponds to reality, as is noted in one dictionary definition: truth is "conformity to fact or actuality."

Within the practice of science, the authority and thus the truth — as far as science can ascertain it — lies in the realm of nature. It does not necessarily lie in any particular human interpretation of what is in this realm. Thus, scientific truth is that which conforms to the reality of nature, as that reality is observed and interpreted by human beings. In this sense, scientific truth which is pragmatic and less than ultimate is found in the content of scientific knowledge and in scientific explanations, generalizations, and laws developed in the building of the body of knowledge which is science. In this way, something is scientifically true if it produces order in past observations and thus has been found to predict correctly the results of further observations. Scientific truth, as viewed in this pragmatic way, consists of perceptions of truth. These perceptions are often very significant and meaningful, though they are always subject to some incompleteness and uncertainty and even to error, and are never absolute in the sense of being ultimate truth.

Some scholars have objected to use of the word truth in this pragmatic sense. How can the word truth, they reason, be used to represent that which is subject to error? Consequently, some philosophers of science prefer to avoid use of the word truth in what we are here designating as pragmatic scientific truth. The differences of judgment on this score are not on the concept of scientific truth or of its importance, but only on the terminology used to describe it.

Recognition that human knowledge and understanding are fallible and may fall short of ultimate and unequivocal truth does not mean that any one viewpoint is as good as another. Thus, for example, the law of gravity and Ohm's Law for direct-current electrical circuitry are both so well established that they invariably merit acceptance with virtually 100% confidence. Other concepts, such as the current, detailed understandings of the physical processes occurring at the center of a galaxy, or deep within the earth that give rise to continental spreading, are accepted with confidence levels that are well under 100% but well over 0%.

Several terms are frequently used in referring to generalized scientific explanations. Let us refer briefly to three — hypothesis, theory, and law. These terms refer to formulations of natural principles based on inference from observed data, but they differ in the relative degree of confidence with which the generalized concept is held.

A hypothesis is a tentative assumption made to test its scientific consequences, but has as yet received little verification or confirmation. A theory is a plausible, scientifically acceptable statement of a general principle, and is used to explain phenomena. A law is a statement of orderliness or interrelationship of phenomena that, as far as is known, is invariable under the stated conditions. However, there is no sharp distinction or dividing line between hypothesis, theory, and law; these terms are not even used consistently in all branches of science. It should be stressed that, contrary to a common misperception, a scientific theory is not a guess. It is an explanation based on observation and confirmed by further observation, though not completely proven in an absolute sense.

Occasional confusion results from the differing usage of the term law in expressing scientific knowledge and in other areas of everyday life. A scientific law, as is a scientific theory, is descriptive rather than prescriptive; it is a statement used to describe regularities found in nature and not a statement of what should happen. It is not correct to consider that natural objects obey the laws of nature; rather, the laws of nature describe the behavior of natural objects. By way of contrast, laws of a human government are prescriptive but not descriptive, in that they prescribe how people should behave but do not necessarily describe how people do behave.

Who are the people who engage in the practice of science? Some are professional scientists, highly educated, trained and experienced in science, but the practice of either field of inquiry is not at all limited to these specialists. Rather, it is an area of human activity for lay people as well as for professional experts. All people can and do observe at least some of that which exists and occurs in the realm of nature and are able to derive some meaning and knowledge, or perception of knowledge, from it.

Let us conclude this very brief discussion of scientific investigation by defining science. Any such definition should provide recognition that science consists in essence of methodology, but that this methodology is inseparable from the subject matter with which it is involved. One useful working definition is this: *science is the body of knowledge obtained by methods based on observation.* Note four implications of this definition. First, the practice of science is a human activity, for it is human beings who do the observing, use the methods, and gain the knowledge. Second, there is an inherent limitation of science, for anything outside of or beyond the senses with which people can observe is, in principle, outside of or beyond the bounds of science. Third, there is an authority in scientific investigation, and that is observation. Fourth, there is a building on the authority, for the methods are based on, not limited to, observation.

In summary, then, in both the scientific study of nature and the study of the Bible, there is a source of input data; it is observation in nature or the writings of the Bible, respectively. Both involve interpretation of those input data, the formulation of generalized statements, and the testing of those generalizations against further input data. Use of the methodologies is a human activity, but the authority lies outside of those humans, in the Bible and in nature, both of which "are there." In both fields, there is work for the scholarly experts and the lay person — for anyone who can read the Bible or who can observe nature through one's senses.

Differences between study of the Bible and study of nature arise from the differing sources of input data. In each case, the subject matter is limited necessarily to that which is contained in the source. Each of the two is thus able to deal with some types of subject matter on which the other is silent, at least in any very direct way. However, there are other areas of subject matter in which both of the sources provide information. It is those subject areas in which both sources provide information that are of concern to us in this book. It may appear that the work of biblical study is completed, because the Old and New Testaments are both complete and have been thus for many centuries. As implied in our discussion of biblical interpretation, however, the study of the Bible is an ongoing process, not only because new generations arise which study it for themselves but also because new evidences concerning it become known, new tools become available for use in studying it, and cultural/linguistic changes occur. At the same time, of course, we recognize that scientific investigation is an ongoing expanding field of study as new techniques and tools of observation become available and as more and more prior knowledge is developed, on which subsequent investigation can be based.

We will use these two sources of information in the next three chapters. Then, in chapter five, we will consider further the basic relationships between the two.

Chapter Two
God Uses Human and Natural Means in Doing What He Does

The purpose of this chapter is to identify a principle regarding how God does what he does. This principle is stated in summary form in the chapter title. It will be restated in more specificity and detail as we proceed through the chapter. This is not the only principle about how God does what he does, but it is a very significant one.

This principle is a special case of a more basic and all-encompassing principle, namely, that God is the Sustainer of all of nature. Thus, the entire realm of nature, including all of its normal and usual components and processes as well as the special and unusual ones, is dependent on God and does not exist apart from him. We will encounter this broader principle again in chapter four, where we will consider the meanings of the terms natural and supernatural.

In this chapter we will consider briefly several different things which are described in the Bible as things which God does or has done, each of which involves action in the realm of nature, and concerning which the Bible provides some information about how it was done. We will include recognition of information from sources other than the Bible, particularly from scientific investigation and observation in nature, when this is appropriate to expand on the biblical explanations of "how" each "it" was done or to relate in any way to them.

The actions of God which are considered in this chapter have been selected in part because they are noncontroversial. By this we mean that they are generally not controversial to people who accept both the Bible and the scientific investigation of nature as sources of information which are valid and reliable, and that there is little or no apparent conflict between the two sources as to the explanations of "how." In the two chapters which follow, we will consider in greater detail two other areas which have often been engulfed in controversy.

Writing of the Bible

The Bible itself presents a twofold claim about the authorship of its component books. First, God himself is the ultimate author and source of these writings. Second, the books were written by human authors. In other words, God did it, but he did so by means of human beings as the direct, immediate authors. Let us now consider briefly, in reverse order, each of these two aspects of the authorship of the Bible and how they fit together.

In many books of the Bible, the human author is identified directly by name, while in others this identification is indirect. In some of the latter and even in some parts of the former, there is uncertainty and/or disagreement among biblical scholars about who the author was, but mostly the authors are fairly well identified and established. However, there is no disagreement arising either from information contained within the Bible or from any source on the conclusion that all of the books had human authorship.

Much is known about most of these authors. They numbered about thirty to forty. They lived and wrote at different times, extending apparently from about 1500 to 400 or so B.C. for the Old Testament books and about 40 to 100 or so A.D. for the New Testament books. These authors varied widely from one another in their cultural, geographic, educational, and vocational characteristics. They did not all use the same language. Some of the later authors may not even have been aware of all the prior books which have since come to be included in the Bible.

The Bible contains many direct and indirect claims to be under the ultimate authorship of God. Whether a reader or interpreter accepts this claim to be valid, there is no room for any substantial disagreement about the fact that the human authors made such a claim both in general and specific ways. For example, many Old Testament sections include the words, "Thus saith the Lord" or the equivalent; according to one count, this occurs over three thousand times in the Old Testament. In John 10:34-35, one part of the Bible is referred to as the "word of God (which) came and … cannot be broken." The phrase, "the word of God" is used repeatedly in referring either to the Bible generally or to some part of it.

The role of God as the ultimate author in the writing of the Bible is described by the term "inspiration." Here we have a source of considerable confusion because this word, like many others, has more than one possible meaning. One dictionary definition of inspiration is, "influence emanating from any object, giving rise to new and elevated thoughts and emotions." In this sense, inspiration is derivable from the physical realm of nature (for example, from standing on the rim and looking out at the Grand Canyon), from an awareness of events and human reactions to them (for example, a person who maintains bravery and cheerfulness in the midst of illness or physical disability may prove inspiring to others), from observing with one's eyes or ears the products of an artist, a musician, or a writer, from being in the "atmosphere" of a political rally or a sporting event before a sellout crowd or in a solemn ceremony or ritual. In this sense, the Bible may be an inspiration to those who read it, and the human authors may have felt inspired when they wrote its books. But this is not at all the thrust of the biblical concept of the inspiration of its writing.

The unique meaning of inspiration as it is used in describing the authorship of the Bible is exemplified by the statement in 2 Peter 1:21, "for no prophecy was ever made by an act of human will, but men moved by the Holy Spirit spoke from

God." This statement includes three points. First, it was men (human beings) who spoke (and wrote). Second, it was not *merely* men who did it. These first two points would appear to be contradictory to each other, were it not for the third — they were moved (that is, carried along or borne along) by the Spirit of God. Thus, God was the Author in the ultimate, basic sense, but he did it by means of certain human beings. The human authors were agents of God in accomplishing the writing of the books which comprise the Bible.

Additional commentary on the meaning of this unique inspiration is to be found in other biblical statements. In 2 Timothy 3:16-17, the word "inspired" appears as the English translation of a Greek word which more literally means "God-breathed:" "All scripture is inspired by God and profitable for teaching, for reproof, for correction, for training in righteousness; that the man of God may be adequate, equipped for every good work." Note also that this particular quotation provides some information to answer the why question as well as the who question. The claimed fact that God is the ultimate author is indicated also in Hebrews 1:1, "God ... spoke long ago to the fathers in the prophets in many portions and in many ways." A further indication that the human authors considered themselves in these writings to be agents of God is provided in 1 Corinthians 2:13, "which things we also speak, not in words taught by human wisdom, but in those taught by the Spirit, combining spiritual thoughts with spiritual words."

This unique meaning of the word inspiration is defined in one dictionary as, "divine influence by which the sacred writers were instructed." Another widely quoted definition states that inspiration is the "special influence of the Holy Spirit guiding persons to write and speak what God communicated, to others, without suspending their individual activity or personality." I suggest that inspiration in this unique sense means that God saw to it that (a) the writers recorded the information he wanted and (b) they did it accurately.

Thus far we have been considering the claimed fact of inspiration but have not discussed the mechanism of it.

Unfortunately, it is often assumed that the mechanism was what might be described as a dictation process, in which the human authors acted in effect as stenographers or as tape recorders, simply writing down what was dictated to them. Much controversy has raged over the years, with one side proclaiming the fact of inspiration and the other side opposing this particular postulated mechanism of inspiration. To build up "straw men" to be knocked down may be a common debating technique, but it is often counterproductive to the identification and resolution of real issues which do exist. It must be stated most emphatically that the dictation mechanism of accomplishing inspiration in the writing of the Bible is definitely not taught by the Bible itself. The individual personalities and styles of the various human authors are very evident. There are varieties of expression, for example, in recordings of the same incident in two or more of the four gospels.

What, then, was the mechanism of inspiration? The Bible itself provides very little information on this point, and most of what is known is quite commonplace and unspectacular as far as any outward evidences are involved. Some authors were personal participants in the historical events about which they wrote, getting their immediate information from their own firsthand experiences. Some authors did research work to obtain their information —- for example, Luke 1:13, "inasmuch as many have undertaken to compile an account of the things accomplished among us, just as those who from the beginning were eyewitnesses and servants of the Word have handed them down to us, *it seemed fitting for me as well, having investigated everything carefully from the beginning, to write it out* for you, in consecutive order, most excellent Theophilus" (italics added). Other writers surely must have shared in what was common knowledge. Some writings of the Bible include information said to have been given to the human authors by direct revelation from God, but even here the mechanisms by which this was accomplished are generally not given in detail.

It seems clear, all-in-all, that the Bible itself stresses very strongly the fact of its unique inspiration, rather than the mechanisms by which this was accomplished.

Thus, in summary, the writing of the Bible is something which God has done, but he has accomplished it by means of human beings as the immediate authors.

Events in the History of Israel

The Old Testament describes the history of the nation Israel. It begins with the patriarchs Abraham, Isaac, and Jacob; goes through the sojourn in Egypt, the exodus, and the eventual return to the homeland just east of the Mediterranean Sea; and ends with the establishment of a kingdom, its division and captivity, and eventually its partial reestablishment at Jerusalem. These biblical accounts provide information about many of God's actions and interactions with Israel, often in considerable detail. We will discuss three things which happened in the history of Israel which are attributed in the Bible to God as the one who did them, and how they were done.

Joseph in Egypt

In Genesis 45 we find that Joseph was in Egypt, in a place of high authority, at a time when his brothers and his father maintained their homes elsewhere. Who caused Joseph to be in Egypt? The answer to this who question is stated clearly, in Joseph's words directed to his brothers, who had come to see him in Egypt: "*for God sent me* before you to preserve life" (Genesis 45:5, italics added). The same answer is repeated in Genesis 45:7 and again in 45:8, "And God sent me before you to preserve for you a remnant in the earth, and to keep you alive by a great deliverance," and "Now, therefore, it was not you who sent me here, but God." So, who caused Joseph to be in Egypt? The biblical answer is that God did. The biblical record in two of these quotations also provides some information about the why question, that is, why God did it.

Next, how did God do it? The Bible itself provides considerable detail about how Joseph came to be in Egypt. In Genesis 37 we find that Joseph's brothers, plotting to kill him, put him in a pit. Then a group of Egyptian travelers came along, to whom the brothers sold Joseph for a sum of twenty shekels of silver. Even with the cultural differences between then and now, we can empathize with much of this sequence of events based on our own awareness of human nature and human activity. So, how was Joseph caused to be in Egypt? The biblical answer is that it was done by human and natural means, much of the detail of which is contained in the biblical record. It is interesting that Genesis 45:8 says that it was not his brothers but God who did it. Yet the brothers in fact were deeply involved in the means by which it happened. So in one very limited sense, it could be concluded that the brothers did it, but in the more ultimate and basic sense it was not the brothers but God who did it.

At the particular time described in Genesis 45, Joseph was in a position of high authority in Egypt. Who put him in this position? The answer is in Genesis 45:9, "God has made me lord of all Egypt." How was it done? The answer is given in considerable detail in the preceding chapters. In Genesis 39:7 we find that Joseph refused to commit adultery with Captain Potiphar's wife, who then framed him in retaliation so that Joseph was placed in prison (verses 8-20). While in prison, Joseph interpreted a dream, which led to being called on to interpret a dream of the Pharaoh, who in return assigned to Joseph his position of authority in Egypt (Genesis 41:39-42). So, who placed Joseph in a position of authority, and how was it done? The biblical answer is that God did it, and that human beings and natural processes were used in doing it.

Israel in the Hands of the Midianites and Amalekites

In Judges 6:1, the history of Israel is picked up at a particular point in historical time with these words: "Then the sons of Israel did what was evil in the sight of the Lord, and

28

the Lord gave them into the hands of Midian seven years." Who gave Israel into the hands of Midian for this seven-year period? The biblical answer is that God (the Lord) did it. How was this done? The next several verses of Judges 6 provide the answer to this how question. Midian exercised its power (verse 2), and in particular the Midianites and Amalekites conducted guerrilla-type warfare both by destroying the Israelites' crops before they were harvested and by killing their livestock (verse 3). So, again we find that the biblical record clearly states that God did something and that human and natural means were used in doing it.

Battle for Jerusalem

In 2 Chronicles 32 and in 2 Kings 19, we have two overlapping accounts of the waging of a particular battle by what was then left of the Southern Kingdom under King Hezekiah and the invading Assyrians, led by their King Sennacherib. This battle was for possession and control of the Southern Kingdom's capital city, Jerusalem. At this point in time, the Northern Kingdom, then called Israel, had fallen into captivity, and what was left of its own government had joined with its conquerors in invading the south, then called Judah. As the battle proceeded, the military situation looked very dark for Judah, but eventually the Assyrians were defeated, and King Hezekiah and his people retained Jerusalem.

Now, let us consider the who question and the how question — who fought the battle for Judah, and how was it done? From 2 Chronicles 32:8 we find that God did it, "with us is *the Lord our God* to help us and *to fight our battles*" (italics added). About how it was done, we find a two-part answer. First, it was done by actions taken by Hezekiah and the people of Judah. They rebuilt the city walls with towers on top to protect their city. They resisted the best they could the military efforts of Sennacherib, for example, in cutting off the water supply and in attempting to wage psychological warfare. Second and in the final analysis the most decisive, it was done by the sudden death one night of 185,000 Assyrians in what is described in 2 Chronicles 32:21 and in 2 Kings 19:35 as direct intervention and involvement of an angel sent by God. The biblical record does not give further detail regarding the means of these deaths. We do not know what the coroner would have written on the death certificates, so to speak, and we have no other sources of information on this point. Conceivably it may have been by means of some deadly microorganisms or infectious disease, as there have been other occasions in history when large numbers of people have died from such causes over short periods of time, or it may have been by some other means which has not been experienced at any other time in human history. We simply do not know. But based on the biblical record we do know that God fought the battle for Judah, and that part, but not necessarily all, of the answer to the how question is that he used natural means in doing so.

These and other events in the history of Israel lead to the conclusions that God was in control throughout the history of Israel, that he often involved human beings and natural processes in very specific ways in exercising his control, and that he acted directly and atypically from time to time. However, we do not have total information of the means by which he did this.

The Incarnation

Who accomplished the plan of salvation, and by what means was it done? The biblical answers to these questions center on the incarnation.

The word incarnation, the root meaning of which is simply "in flesh," is defined in the dictionary as "the embodiment of a deity or spirit in some form of earthly existence" or "the union of divinity with humanity in Jesus Christ." Thus, the term incarnation refers to what the Bible teaches to be the fact that God himself, in the person of the eternal Son, became human at a particular time in history.

That Jesus was truly God is indicated, for example, by John 1:1, "In the beginning was the Word, and the Word was with God, and the Word was God." That the title "Word" refers to Jesus and that Jesus was truly human are indicated later in the same chapter, in John 1:14, "And the Word became flesh and dwelt among us." The deity and the humanity of Jesus are referred to together in Romans 8:3, "… God did, sending His own son in the likeness of sinful flesh … ," and in 1 Timothy 3:16, "And by common confession great is the mystery of godliness. He who was revealed in the flesh was vindicated in the Spirit, beheld by angels, proclaimed among the nations, believed on in the world, taken up into glory." The deity and the humanity of Jesus are combined in one of the names used in the Bible to refer to him, Immanuel, which means "God with us."

Some biblical references to Jesus stress the fact that he was the eternal God, even while he was temporarily in human form. One such statement is in Colossians 2:9, "For in Him all the fullness of deity dwells in bodily form." Another is in Jesus' own words, John 10:30, "I and the father are one." Some people have interpreted this statement to mean "one in purpose," but to do so is to disregard the context. The next verse indicates that the Jews responded by taking up stones to stone him, a clear indication that he had in fact claimed to be God. Along a similar line, Jesus several times claimed the authority to forgive sins, a prerogative which he and the Jews among whom he ministered fully recognized to be a claim to be God. In Matthew 9:2-3, for example, Jesus made this claim, which would have been blasphemy, as his accusers took it to be, were it not true.

Other biblical references to Jesus stress the fact of his humanity. People from his home area, knowing that he had been raised from birth in the family of Mary and Joseph, recognized him as a fellow human being, as in Matthew 13:55, "Is not this the carpenter's son? Is not His mother called Mary, and His brothers, James and Joseph and Simon and Judas?" Although the biblical record includes only a little information about his childhood years and experiences, it does summarize them in Luke 2:52, "And Jesus kept increasing in wisdom and stature, and in favor with God and man." In his adult years, about which we have much more information, he was like other human beings in that he ate, slept, had friends, got tired, and eventually died.

The birth of Jesus was like that of all other human beings, in that his mother Mary became pregnant and in due time delivered the baby. The birth differed from that of all other human beings, in that conception occurred of the Holy Spirit and not of a human male, as indicated for example in Isaiah 7:14, "Therefore the Lord Himself will give you a sign: Behold a virgin will be with child and bear a son, and she will call His name Immanuel," and in Matthew 1:20, "Joseph, son of David, do not be afraid to take Mary as your wife, for that which has been conceived in her is of the Holy Spirit."

The death of every human being is by means of some natural or inflicted causes, and the death of Jesus was no exception. Unlike other deaths, however, Jesus' death was followed by his resurrection from the dead. His life between birth and death differed from that of every other human being in that he did not sin: "Who committed no sin, nor was any deceit found in His mouth" (1 Peter 2:22).

In the incarnation, we find a unique and total combination of the transcendence and immanence of God. However, the Bible does not merely teach the fact of the incarnation. It also teaches the purpose of it, and that was to accomplish the plan of salvation. This was the culmination toward which Old Testament events had been moving ever since the early chapters of Genesis, and it is the historical, factual basis on which subsequent New Testament events are based. To return to our questions at the beginning of this section, who accomplished the plan of salvation, and by what means was it done? God did it, and he did it by means of the incarnation. The incarnation involved human and natural processes, and it also involved processes which have not been seen in any other case before or since.

Events in the
New Testament Church

Much of the Old Testament consists of descriptions of things which God did in and through the nation Israel. Similarly, the New Testament consists in part of descriptions of things which God did in and through the Christian church during a period of several decades in the first century A.D. The book of Acts surveys this history, and the epistles provide much additional information about it.

The growth of the early Christian church was very rapid and widespread, beginning with the Day of Pentecost as described in Acts 2 and continuing through the entire period described in the New Testament. This rapid growth occurred in the midst of considerable difficulty and open hostility. From within Judaism came persistent opposition. Christianity had arisen from within Judaism and was in competition with the various sects which comprised Judaism at that time. Also, the Christian movement quickly branched out to the acceptance of Gentiles, a step which caused further dismay and opposition from Judaism. Continual opposition came also from pagan society for a variety of apparent reasons: fear of the Christians because they sometimes met in secret, accusations of atheism because the early Christians opposed festivals and other acts which signified allegiance to pagan gods, fears of the potential political and economic influences of the expanding church, and accusations of anti-intellectualism. It is interesting that these same sources of opposition to the Christian church are not unknown even today.

The remarkably rapid growth of the early Christian church is historical fact. Who was responsible for it? The biblical answer to this question is that God did it. One direct statement to this effect is given in Acts 2:47, "And the Lord was adding to their number day by day those who were being saved."

Now, consider this question: how did God accomplish it? The biblical answer to this question is that God used human beings, processes, and events in the realm of nature to accomplish this growth. Several "sermons" which are excerpted in the book of Acts, and which were followed by or accompanied by many people becoming believers and thus church members, were delivered by human beings and were based on the historical facts of the incarnation, and the life, death, and resurrection of Jesus. The joining together of God as the one who did it and various human beings as the agents of God in accomplishing it is illustrated by 1 Corinthians 3:6-7, "I (Paul) planted, Apollos watered, but God was causing the growth. So then neither the one who plants nor the one who waters is anything, but God who causes the growth."

Human beings and events and processes in nature were involved in varying ways in the conversions of individuals as described in the New Testament. The biblical teaching is clear that salvation is singularly in Jesus Christ alone but that the avenue through which different individuals approach him vary from one case to another. As described in Acts 9, and repeated elsewhere, the conversion of Saul involved at least two of his five natural senses — he saw a bright, blinding light and he heard the voice of the Lord speaking to him (others with him heard the voice but apparently did not make out the words). Two more of his senses were involved indirectly or soon after that — his sense of touch as he fell to the ground and his sense of taste as he went without food for three days.

A less dramatic conversion was that of the Ethiopian eunuch as described in Acts 8. This gentleman was reading from the Scripture but not fully comprehending what he read. Then Philip, serving as a teacher and one-on-one preacher explained the Old Testament readings by relating them to Jesus, whereon the Ethiopian came to believe with all his heart. This type of conversion is perhaps quite typical in some ways of many others in New Testament times and ever since. The important role of human beings in enabling other human beings to know Jesus is indicated in Romans 10:14, "How then shall they call upon Him in whom they have not believed? And how shall they believe in Him whom they have not heard? And how shall they hear without a preacher?"'

So, who caused the remarkable growth of the Christian church in New Testament times, and by what means was it done? God did it, and in so doing he used human beings, processes, and events in the realm of nature. The Christian church has been continuing and growing ever since, and these answers to the who question and the how question remain the same.

Birth and Death of the Individual Human Being

Scientific investigations have led to considerable detailed knowledge and understanding in the area of human reproduction. The Bible, too, is a source of information on the birth of the individual human being. It does so both in statements about some specific human beings and in other statements generally applicable to all births.

In Genesis 17:16 and 19 are words of the Lord to Abraham concerning his wife Sarah and the birth of Isaac, "And I will bless her, and indeed I will give you a son by her ... Sarah your wife shall bear you a son." Note that (a) God is the one who is providing the birth of Isaac ("indeed I will give you a son") and (b) the birth will be accomplished by the normal reproductive means applicable to all human births ("by her" and "Sarah shall bear you a son"). Thus, the ultimate "who" and the immediate "how" are joined closely together in the birth of Isaac.

A similar situation is described concerning the birth of Samuel. Here God is identified as the who in 1 Samuel 1:27, "For this boy I prayed, and the Lord has given me my petition which I asked of Him." And the "how" is identified quite specifically in 1 Samuel 1:19-20, "And Elkanah had relations with Hannah his wife ... and it came about in due time, after Hannah had conceived, that she gave birth to a son."

A third example is found in Job 1:21, "And he (Job) said, naked I came from my mother's womb, and naked I shall return there. The *Lord gave and the Lord has taken away*. Blessed be the name of the Lord" (italics added). This statement includes full recognition that natural means and processes are involved, and yet it specifically identifies God as the one who gives life to the individual human being. This verse is a quotation from Job, but the next verse effectively indicates that God is endorsing it. While the context refers specifically to Job, the portion italicized above has long been widely interpreted as applying not only to Job but much more generally to all individual human beings.

The death of the individual human being is similar to the birth, in that it is describable by some mechanism based on information obtainable from scientific investigation in the realm of nature and, at the same time, it is somehow within God's actions as the ultimate "who." Refer again to Job 1:21, "... The Lord gave and the Lord has taken away ... " The Bible, along with its identification of God as the one who takes life away, describes in varying detail the mechanisms by which various individual human beings have met death — some from wounds suffered in battle, some from hunger and malnutrition, some from accidents, some after extended illness, some in youth, and others in old age. The dual recognition that it is God who takes away life and that some medical mechanisms are involved are frequently made in Christian funeral services today, with the reading of the quotation cited above from Job 1:21, even when the coroner's report or the physician's statement on the death certificate identifies specifically what the cause of death was.

As it is with the birth and the death of the individual human being, so it is with his or her life in-between birth and death. The Bible teachings recognize fully that human life proceeds, at least in considerable measure, by means of natural processes, but these teachings also identify God as the one who makes and sustains all of life including these natural processes. The general "flavor" of biblical teachings in this area is indicated by Psalms 118:24, "This is the day which the Lord has made; Let us rejoice and be glad in it"; by Acts 17:25, "He Himself gives to all life and breath and all things"; by Isaiah 42:5, "Thus says God the Lord, who created the heavens and stretched them out, who spread out the earth and its vege-tation, who gives breath to the people on it, and spirit to those who walk in it"; and by Matthew 5:45, "for He causes His sun to rise on the evil and the good, and sends rain on the righteous and the unrighteous." Surely we have considerable reliable information obtained by the scientific investigation of nature on the means about how each new day follows from the one before, how breath is given to the individual human being, how the sun rises, and how rain develops in clouds and falls to the earth. Knowledge obtained from the study of the Bible does not contradict this scientific knowledge. It cor-roborates it where there is overlap and supplements it with additional knowledge, especially in the area of the "who" as contrasted to the "how." In chapter three we will consider in greater detail information gained from the Bible and from the scientific study of nature about the role of God in the origins and in the continuation of the realm of nature, including man.

Another important factor arises in considering the life of the individual human being, who is a Christian through faith in Jesus Christ as personal Savior and Lord. For this person there is an even more intimate relationship between God and the life of that individual, as is described in Galatians 2:20, "I have been crucified with Christ; and it is no longer I who live, but Christ lives in me; and the life which I now live in the flesh I live by faith in the son of God, who loved me and delivered Himself up for me."

So, who causes the birth and the death of the individual human being and provides and sustains the life in-between? The biblical answer is that God does it. But how does God do it? The biblical answer here has several components, one of which is that he does it by means of common and generally well-known natural processes.

Relationship of the "Who" to the "How"

In this chapter we have considered several things which are identified in the Bible as things which God has done. For each, the Bible includes some information about how it was done, and this has included in each case the use of natural processes and mechanisms. For some, additional information can be obtained from sources of information other than the study of the Bible, including scientific investigation in the realm of nature, about how it could have been done or how similar situations and actions might be accomplished. The items considered in this chapter have been among those in which there has been relatively little conflict involving overlapping information obtained from biblical and extra-biblical sources of information, at least as both are generally interpreted and understood.

In each of these items it is readily possible to study the "how" without accepting the biblical conclusions about the "who." Accordingly one can study in detail, and even with considerable respect, the content written in the Bible without agreeing with the biblical claim that God did it. Or one can "explain" the events in the history of Israel and in the life of Christ, or in the New Testament church, or in the birth and death of individual human beings without accepting the biblical claim that God "is there" and that he did it. Alternative explanations of the "who" are always conceivable, even among people who agree on the "how." These alternatives may arise from a denial of God, or from an agnostic attitude (that is, "I do not know") toward the existence or nature of God, or from being satisfied with a more immediate and less-than-ultimate viewpoint in the areas represented by the question of "who."

Recognizing the rational conceivability of these alternatives, we should guard closely against a very serious danger — we must not extrapolate from knowledge of a natural mechanism for something to a denial of the biblical concept of God. There has unfortunately been a tendency for many people to assume that a concept of God is valid and useful only in the absence of a human or natural explanation for anything. It is for this reason that, in earlier times and in some cultures, phenomena such as thunder and lightning were attributed to a deity in the absence of known natural explanations for their occurrence, with subsequent discarding of any recognition of God's involvement when the physical causes of thunder and lightning became known. Thus, the concept of a deity has been that of a gap-filler, to be called on to explain things that could not be explained otherwise. Assuming this to be the proper concept of God, there is a tendency to extrapolate from knowledge of a natural mechanism for something to a denial of the claim that God did it. It should be stated most emphatically, however, that the God of the Bible is not a "God-of-the-gaps," and that the God of the Bible is both transcendent to the realm of nature, with all the matter and processes which comprise that realm, and immanent within that realm. He is transcendent to the means which he uses in doing what he does, and he is immanent within those means.

Another danger which we should guard against is to conclude that rational knowledge of the means by which these things are accomplished provides unequivocal or absolute proof either that the biblical claim that God did it is correct or that this claim is wrong. A fair, rational study of any of the items selected for comment in this chapter can provide powerful supporting evidence that the God of the Bible exists and that "he did it." This type of evidence may even seem overwhelming to one who already believes and accepts the Bible as authoritative, as I do. But other people, who approach the detailed study of any of these items with atheistic or agnostic presuppositions, can quite rationally conclude from the same knowledge of "how" that alternative explanations of "who" provide supporting evidence for their basic views.

A third danger to be guarded against is that of considering that any established, verified explanation from the realm of nature is complete. Even within the realm of nature, we do not really know that our knowledge of anything is complete. This is true with respect to biblically-generated knowledge concerning natural phenomena. For example, we do not know what the precise cause of death was for the 185,000 Assyrians mentioned earlier, although the biblical record identifies that it was God who caused it to happen. The incompleteness of knowledge is also true with respect to knowledge obtained by the scientific investigation of nature, as is inherent in the basic methodology of what science is. Furthermore, recognizing that God is transcendent to nature as well as immanent in it, it is surely possible for him to vary from what are commonly thought of as normal processes and events within nature. Clearly he did this, for example, in the conception of the man Jesus and in his resurrection. So, for one to have knowledge of a natural means for something to have been done does not necessarily indicate that one has total knowledge, not even total knowledge within the realm of nature.

God does use human and natural means in doing what he does. He is the Creator and the Sustainer of nature. He is not limited to the use of what are normally considered natural processes. We will return to these considerations of the relationship of the "who" to the "what" in subsequent chapters.

Chapter Three

What About Origins of the Universe and the Earth, of Life, of Man?

The topics of origins of the universe and the earth, of life, and of man have probably received more attention than any other one in which information is derivable both from the Bible and from the scientific study of nature. Much of this attention has been engulfed in conflict, often with emotional as well as intellectual overtones. There have been variations in interpretations of what the Bible has to say about these topics, in understandings derived from scientific observations in the realm of nature, and in comparing information obtained from the two sources. Differences are encountered in dealing with who, when, and how questions about the origins of the universe, the first living matter, and the first human beings.

One practical consequence of these conflicts has been the tendency for some people to reject science, or at least the validity of the practice of science by scientists, in the name of the Bible or, conversely, to reject the reliability of the Bible in the name of science. In my judgment, this is particularly unfortunate because much of the conflict has resulted from pseudo-issues rather than from the real issues which do exist. First, there has been a tendency to blur the distinction between what is interpreted and the interpretation of it, both in the study of the Bible and in the scientific investigation of nature. Second, there has been a mixing together of the questions of who and how in dealing with origins. Third, there has been a tendency to extrapolate from a particular answer to who to demand a particular answer to how, and vice versa.

Our purpose in this chapter is neither to review the history of these conflicts nor to marshal the wide range of evidences which may have bearing on the subject. It is our purpose to consider in summary form the relevant knowledge obtainable both from the Bible and from the scientific investigation of nature; and to provide a valid perspective for viewing both the distinctives and the overlappings of these two sources of information about origins. Hopefully this approach will facilitate the identification of what the real problems are and thus help in avoiding unnecessary conflicts and polarizations over pseudo-issues.

Information from the Bible

The Bible provides much information which bears on several aspects of the subject of origins. If the Bible indeed is the inspired and authoritative Word of God, as we are taking it to be, then there is no reason to assume that its coverage has to be limited to any particular aspect of origins. God could have revealed anything about origins that he chose to reveal in the Bible in as much or as little detail as he desired. Therefore, in seeking information from the Bible we are limited not by what God could have included in it, but by what he did include in it. In dealing with origins, the Bible does reveal clearly the answer to the question of who did it, and it provides some information relating to other questions such as how and why.

The Who Question

With respect to the who question about origins, the biblical answer is that God did it all. It is stated directly in several places and indirectly indicated in many others that the universe and the earth and all that they contain, including life and man, were created by God. The first verse of the Bible, Genesis 1:1 states: "In the beginning God created the heavens and the earth." Other relevant statements include Isaiah 45:12 and 18, "It is I who made the earth, and created man upon it, I stretched out the heavens with my hands, and I ordained all their host" and "For thus says the Lord, who created the heavens (He is the God who formed the earth and made it, He established it and did not create it a waste place, But formed it to be inhabited); I am the Lord, and there is none else"; Psalm 102:25, "Of old Thou didst found the earth; and the heavens are the work of thy hands"; Psalm 89:11 and 12, "The heavens are Thine, the earth also is Thine; The world and all it contains, Thou hast founded them; the north and the south, Thou hast created them ..."; John 1:3, "All things came into being through Him; and apart from Him nothing came into being that has come into being"; Acts 17:24, "... God, who created all things"; Colossians 1:16, "For in Him all things were created, both in the heavens and on earth, visible and invisible, whether thrones or dominions or rulers or authorities — all things have been created through Him and for Him."

The When Question

The most basic factor in a consideration of information obtained from the Bible about origins is that there indeed was a beginning. There are differences of understanding about biblical teaching on just how long ago this beginning was, but there is no question at all that the Bible clearly indicates that the realm of nature, of matter and energy, of space and time did have a beginning and has not been in existence from eternity past. Refer again, for example, to Genesis 1:1, "In the beginning God created ..."

Turning more specifically to the question of when this beginning was, we find that there are differences of understanding about just what the Bible teaches — is the earth young, created and populated in six 24-hour days about 6,000 or so years ago, or is it much older, created long ago and populated over long periods of time? Biblical evidences on this topic are interpreted both ways by people who accept the Bible as authoritative. Much of the difference centers on the meaning of the word "day" in Genesis 1 and 2.

In every place where the word day appears in these chapters and in most other places in the Old Testament, it is a translation of the Hebrew word *yome* (this and other Hebrew words will be written in this chapter in equivalent English letters). The uses of this word in the first chapter appear to fall into two groups, both of which are illustrated in Genesis 1:5. The first one, "And God called the light day, and the darkness he called night," signifies a time of light as contrasted to darkness. The second one, "And there was evening and there was morning, one day," signifies a larger period of time which in context appears to include more than the first one. The first usage is found also in Genesis 1:14, 16, and 18, and the second in Genesis 1:8, 13, 19, 23, and 31. These two meanings of day could conceivably be equivalent to the period between sunrise and sunset, and a twenty-four-hour period, respectively. However, this interpretation is rendered less than certain by two considerations: the sun, moon, and stars are identified for the first time in Genesis 1:14 on the fourth of the six days; in Genesis 2:4, the word day, which is the Hebrew *yome*, is used as equivalent to the sum of all six of the days in the first chapter.

Other usages of the Hebrew *yome*, translated by the English day, fall generally into three groups. First, *yome* can mean the period of light between sunrise and sunset, as in Genesis 31:39, " … whether stolen by day or by night." Second, *yome* can mean a 24-hour period, as Genesis 34:25, "Now it came about on the third day …" Third, *yome* can mean time, without reference either to daylight or a 24-hour period, as Genesis 27:2, "And Isaac said, Behold now, I am old and I do not know the day of my death," and also Psalm 20:1, "May the Lord answer you in the day of trouble."

The Hebrew word *yome* is not always translated into the English as day. For example, it may be age, as in Genesis 18:11, "Now Abraham and Sarah were old, advanced in age … ," and also in Genesis 24:1, "Now Abraham was old, advanced in age." And *yome* may also be translated as time or even as long time, as in Genesis 26:8, "And it came about, when he had been there a long time …" Clearly it would not be incorrect to translate *yome* either as a period between sunrise and sunset or as a 24-hour period in any of these instances. We conclude, then, that the Hebrew word *yome* can mean a period of daylight, a 24-hour period, or a longer, indefinite period of time. The immediate context in the first chapter of Genesis may not totally prove which of these three is intended, but that it likely is the longer, indefinite period of time is substantiated by the two considerations mentioned above, the fact that the sun is not identified until the fourth *yome* or day, and the fact the *yome* in Genesis 2:4 is equivalent to the sum of all of the *yomes* of the first chapter.

In summary, then, many people who strongly affirm their full agreement with the biblical view that the God of the Bible is the Creator of the universe, interpret biblical evidence as favoring the old earth view. Others interpret the biblical evidences differently. Contrary to the claims of some of the latter group of Bible believers, the interpretation of biblical evidences to favor the old earth view is not a recent effort to reinterpret the Bible to make it fit in with modern scientific viewpoints. Some leading church fathers of many centuries ago, including Iraneous, Origen, Augustine, and Thomas Aquinas, all endorsed the view that the days of Genesis 1 and 2 were long periods of time.

The How Question

With respect to the question of how God created, the Bible provides relatively little information, but it does provide some. Some of this information is subject to varying interpretations which are at some points contradictory to each other. One concept is simply that God spoke a word and the created item or being appeared. The Bible does include such statements as "Then God said ... and it was so," in Genesis 1:14-15 and in Genesis 1:24, for example. But these statements identify who did it, and do not describe how it was done. An analogous usage of terminology is common in describing actions occurring in the human realm. For example, with respect to a jail sentence for a law violator, a judge speaks and the order is accomplished. With respect to a business venture, the president of a firm speaks, and it is done. With respect to implementing standby wage and price controls, the appropriate governmental official speaks (orally or in writing) and it is done. For each of these indicated actions, the statements identify who caused it to be done but really do not describe the means by which it was accomplished. In general, whenever a person who has (a) the authority and (b) the control of means to enforce that authority, "speaks," it is done. So it is really a misinterpretation of the Bible to conclude that, because "God said … and it was so," there is nothing further to consider about how it was accomplished.

An insight into biblical teaching on the how of origins can be gained by noting the meanings of three words: create, make, and form as they are used in various grammatical forms in the biblical account of origins. Problems of interpretation which are relevant to our present considerations center on whether the actions represented by these words occurred instantaneously or if natural processes were employed to any significant extent. Let us examine these three words with this point in mind.

The word create appears in one or another of its English forms in Genesis 1:1, 21, 27 (3 times) and in 2:3, 4. In each instance the Hebrew word is *bara*, which is the only Hebrew root word which is translated as create, created, createth, or Creator anywhere in the Old Testament. In all of these usages the subject of the verb is God. The object may be concrete, as man in Genesis 1:27, or abstract, as a clean heart in Psalm 51:10. The word *bara* itself does not necessarily imply whether the action is instantaneous, but if there be any context at all for the statement in Genesis 1:1, it is the rest of the chapter, in which case Genesis 1:1 is a summary statement of the overall creation process. The creative act to which it refers took place over the period of time represented by the six days of creation. Genesis 1:21 is not clear by itself about whether process was involved, but the contexts in verses 20 and 22 imply that natural processes indeed were involved. The three uses of create in verse 27 do not clearly imply whether the indicated action was accomplished instantaneously or through some process. However, the prior verse used the word make in referring to the same action, and the two words create and make are used as if they are interchangeable in Genesis 2:3 and 4.

The word make, in its various grammatical forms, is from the Hebrew word *asah*. It appears in Genesis 1:7, 16 (twice), 25, 26, 31, and 2:3, 4, 18. In addition, in Genesis 2:2 (twice) *asah* is translated done in the New American Standard Bible and made in the King James, in Genesis 2:7 it is formed in both versions, and in Genesis 2:22 as fashioned or made in the two versions, respectively. An analysis of these and other Old Testament usages of *asah* reveals that its subject varies widely, and that the action often does involve natural processes and materials.

The word formed which appears in Genesis 2:7, 8 and 2:19, is from the Hebrew *yatsar*, the root meaning of which is to form by molding or squeezing into shape as a potter working with clay. This literal meaning is indeed the actual meaning in at least some Old Testament usages of *yatsar* as, for example, Isaiah 44:10, which refers to the forming or fashioning of a graven image. In this and many other instances, the context makes it clear that the action was accomplished not instantaneously, but by using natural processes. The statement in Genesis 2:7 may not in itself be so clear-cut on this point, but there is implication that this action, also, involved natural processes in the references to dust of the ground and to breathing.

The three terms, *bara, asah,* and *yatsar* are all used in grammatical constructions which are parallel and seemingly interchangeable in a statement in Isaiah 43:7 referring to God's relationship to the Jewish people: "Everyone who is called by my name, and whom I have created for my glory, whom I have formed, even whom I have made."

In summary, the three verbs used to describe God's actions in accomplishing the origins of the earth, the universe, life, and humans do not at all rule out the possibility that natural processes were involved once the realm of nature had been brought into existence. It must be emphasized here that we are not attempting to define or describe what God could have done, but rather to understand the proper interpretation of the biblical account of what God did do.

Unique Place of Human Beings in Creation

The biblical account of creation includes consideration of the origins of the earth and the universe, the waters and the lands on the surface of the earth, vegetation, sea and land animals, birds, and human beings. In all of this, God is the Creator, and the entire realm of nature is created, including humankind. God is eternal, already being in existence "in the beginning," while the realm of nature is temporal in that it did have a beginning. However, in all of creation humans are in a unique position as established by God.

The uniqueness of people as indicated by the Bible is three-fold. First, they are the only part of nature which is described as being created in the image and likeness of God, Genesis 1:26a, 27a, "Then God said, Let us make man in our image, according to our likeness ... And God created man in His own image, in the image of God He created him." Human beings comprise the only part of animate nature whose creation is described as being that of a living soul, Genesis 2:7, "Then the Lord God formed man ... and breathed into his nostrils the breath of life; and man became a living being (soul)." We will not attempt to describe here the full meaning of these state-ments. However, they surely do point to a uniqueness in con-trast to all the rest of creation. Other parts of the Bible provide much further detail on the meaning and significance of this feature.

A second aspect of this uniqueness is in the relationship of humans to the rest of the realm of nature. Human beings are a part of nature and have the assignment from God to exercise jurisdiction over the rest of nature. Genesis 1:28, "And God blessed them; and God said to them, Be fruitful and multiply, and fill the earth, and subdue it; and rule over the fish of the sea and over the birds of the sky, and over every living thing that moves on the earth." This does not mean, of course, that people are to exploit the rest of nature selfishly, but rather that they have the God-given responsibility to exercise this jurisdiction as a trust from God who created it all.

The third aspect of this uniqueness in all of creation lies in the area of sin and guilt. The biblical account of creation leads directly into consideration of the origin and the meaning of sin and its consequences, and much of the rest of the Bible deals with this general topic. In this area, human beings are unique among all the rest of that which God created as described in the first two chapters of Genesis.

Information from the Scientific Investigation of Nature

The scientific investigation of nature has brought within human knowledge tremendous amounts of information concerning the realm of matter and energy and the laws which describe their actions and interactions. The rate of acquisition of this knowledge has accelerated rapidly over the years, so much so that a large fraction of all the scientific knowledge which man now has, has been gained within the lifetimes of people now alive. This seemingly does not mean that we are rapidly approaching a point of complete knowledge of the realm of nature. It appears that the more we know about nature the more conscious we are that there is much more that we do not know. To say that we humans have complete scientific explanation in any particular area is in effect to say that we have stopped asking questions about it.

Faced on the one hand with the considerable knowledge of nature which now exists and on the other hand with the awareness of how much more there is to be known, we are confronted with an awareness of the vastness of size, time and masses of matter, as well as the tremendous magnitude of the ranges within each. It is probably inevitable that this awareness has led to widespread interest in the scientific questions about when it all began and how it all came into being. Whether this is inevitable or not, the history of science reveals that these questions have been of active interest throughout recorded history up to and including the present time. What then can scientific investigation tell us about the times and the processes of the origins of the earth, the universe, life, and humans?

The Who Question

Science per se can provide no basic knowledge about the who of origins. Scientific investigation is inherently limited to the what and the how. To be sure, scientists and other human beings may extrapolate from their scientific observations of nature to seek support for whatever their concepts might be about the who question of origins. For example, people who by faith have adopted a theistic viewpoint or who are at least open toward it, may find support in nature for that viewpoint. One who believes in God may in all sincerity see in nature something of God's glory, as declared in Psalm 19:1, "The heavens are telling of the glory of God; and the firmament is declaring the work of His hands." At the same time, other people who deny such a theistic viewpoint or who are at least skeptical of it, may find support for their nontheistic or agnostic viewpoints when they consider the results of scientific investigations as they relate to origins. The latter tendency is particularly in evidence if the theistic viewpoint is assumed to be that of a God-of-the-gaps, in which God is taken to be relevant only as an explanation wherever there are gaps in the scientific, naturalistic explanations of that which exists. However, these considerations in either direction are actually extensions from one's own assumptions and conceptual framework and are not science per se.

It should be noted also that science likewise is unable to provide any basic knowledge about the why of origins. Scientists have frequently engaged themselves in speculation and in controversy over teleology — about purpose in nature —

but they do so not as scientists but as human beings who are not restricted in their reasoning processes to that which is immediately or strictly scientific.

The When Question

One of the most basic components of this information is that many evidences point toward the definite conclusion that there were origins, that the universe and the earth as they now exist are not permanent but that they are the results of changes that had their beginning in time. Indeed, it has been possible to extrapolate backward in time from scientific observations today to derive the approximate times at which the origins presumably occurred.

Present knowledge about the approximate age of the solar system and the earth is based on several different types of scientific investigation which are in varying degrees independent of each other. Foremost among these are methods based on measurements of the radioactive decay of certain elements in rocks. From measurements of the present composition of rocks in terms of the products of such decay, along with experimental determinations of the rates at which the processes occur, it is possible to calculate the apparent ages of the rock samples. There are several different chains of radioactive decay processes which are largely independent physically and chemically from each other, and which are useful for measuring the ages of rocks which are found in nature. Some of these techniques lead to minimum ages and others to maximum ages. There are possible errors in these determinations, but careful experimental design and performance can minimize them and provide some indication of the probable magnitude and direction of residual errors. Furthermore, some sources of possible uncertainty can be minimized by conducting the measurements on meteorites and on rocks brought back to earth from the moon.

Other scientific techniques used for the determination of the age of the earth and the solar system include those based on measurement of the salt content of the oceans and the rates at which additions are being made to it. Another technique involves measuring the movements of the moon relative to the earth. Yet another consists experimentally of measurement of the rate of energy emission from the sun. To be sure there are uncertainties in all of these techniques for determining the age of the earth and the solar system. Many of these potential errors are identifiable and statistically quantifiable. Of particular significance, however, is the conclusion that the several distinctly different types of investigation are in general agreement in pointing to an origin of the earth and the solar system in the order of six billion years ago. The precise value of this figure is not important to our considerations in this book, but the general magnitude of it is.

By adding to the foregoing types of scientific investigation some additional ones, it is possible to derive an approximate age for the overall universe of which our solar system is but a small part. Much of this additional information is derived from measurements on the spectral distributions and intensities of light coming to earth from distant stars in our galaxy and from other galaxies. Scientific measurement is not limited to visible light, but can include other electromagnetic radiation as well. The figure for the age of the universe, derived as a composite from many measurements and their interpretations is of the order of fifteen billion years. Again the precise value of the figure is not significant to our present concerns. Nevertheless, scientific evidences point now to an age of the universe of this general order of magnitude.

Scientific investigations of the ages of life and human beings on earth, like those of the earth itself, have included more than one type of work. One is based on measurements of radioactive decay processes. Some of these processes occur at rates such that they are useful for dating objects much younger than the earth itself, and they are appropriate for determining the ages of objects that have been alive in the past or which have been associated in some way with objects that were alive. Another very significant part of the scientific investigation of the ages of living things on the earth is that which is based on the fossil record which has been left behind by objects that were once alive. No precise dates can be established from scientific evidences about when life first appeared on earth. However, it should suffice for our present purposes to note that scientific studies indicate that life probably has been present for at least one-third of the total age of the earth and that it may have been here for much longer than that.

With respect to the time when man first appeared on earth, scientific evidences include those involved in the science of anthropology in addition to some of the types of study mentioned above. Cultural features are helpful in this regard, including, for example, tools made by early man. Man is much younger than numerous other forms of life on earth, according to the results of scientific investigations, but there is still much uncertainty about how long man has lived on earth. Indeed, this is a very active field of contemporary research. For our present purposes, suffice it to say that humans in the modern anatomical form have apparently been around for one hundred thousand years or so, certainly not only for a few thousand years nor for a few billion years.

The How Question

When we turn to the question of the how of origins, we find that much information is provided by the scientific investigation of nature. One of the most basic components of this information is that many scientific evidences point to the definite conclusion that there were origins, that the universe and the earth as they now exist are not permanent but are the results of changes that had their beginnings in time.

Let us refer now to the scientific discipline commonly referred to as cosmology. According to one dictionary definition, "Cosmology is the area of science aimed at a comprehensive theory of the creation, evolution and present structure of the entire physical universe." Note that cosmology is an area of science and that its subject matter content has considerable breadth and depth. It deals with the beginning of the entire physical universe, with changes which have occurred in it since that beginning, and with its present structure. In brief, cosmology deals with the entire realm of nature, that is, with the realm of matter and energy, space and time.

Serious reflection on this definition immediately brings to mind a very basic question. Is the totality of all that is incorporated within "the creation, evolution and present structure of the entire physical universe" explainable either in principle or in present actuality by means of scientific explanation? Or to put it differently, is it possible for any scientific explanation, which consists of statements of cause-and-effect relationships within the realm of nature, to deal comprehensively with such a broad range of subject matter?

This question reaches beyond the bounds of science, so it is not strictly a scientific question. Some would answer in the affirmative — yes, it is possible because there is no reality beyond the bounds of that which is matter and energy. Others would answer in the negative — no, it is not possible because there is reality which is not explainable in terms of cause-and-effect relationships strictly within the bounds of the realm of nature. This question is not fully a scientific one, and it is not one of science versus the Bible. It is a question about the difference between basic world views, a topic to which we will return in chapter five.

It is possible, even inevitable, for human beings to extrapolate beyond the purely scientific in dealing with the subject matter of cosmology and thereby to draw conclusions on, for example, the existence or non-existence of a supreme being. For this reason, it is helpful to refer to the strictly scientific aspects of cosmology as scientific cosmology, whether or not one agrees that this covers the totality of all within the creation, evolution, and present structure of the entire physical universe.

Scientific cosmology has gone through several stages throughout human history. For ages the dominant assumption was that of an earth-centered universe. This was eventually replaced by the Copernican view, based on the acceptance of the idea of a heliocentric (sun-centered) universe. The latter view was directly contradictory to the earlier one, at least in this one central feature. Much later, it became clear that scientific evidences indicated that the Milky Way was a galaxy consisting of many stars far apart from each other. Much of the detail of the heliocentric view remained intact for the solar system, even after it was realized that the solar system was but a small portion of the universe. Then, in the twentieth century, additional galaxies were discovered at still greater distances.

How does scientific cosmology today account for the origin of such a vast universe? The most widely accepted scientific model is the "big bang model," according to which all matter and energy were at some instant in the past concentrated in a small space, which exploded some fifteen billion years or so ago and has been expanding ever since. However, to describe the big bang in this way is to oversimplify it greatly.

A more detailed, scientific explanation of the big bang involves the scientific concepts of relativity and quantum mechanics, which in turn are based heavily on mathematical considerations and are not readily amenable to descriptive terminology. For example, space and time are not considered in relativity concepts as separate entities but as components of a single four-dimensional universe. And matter and energy are viewed in quantum mechanics not as separate "things" but as manifestations of some entities which are fundamental to both of them. Within this framework of thought, the actual bang is not considered simply as an explosion at some point in space, but as the beginning of the space-time four-dimensional universe, and not solely or separately as a beginning of matter, energy, space, or time.

With respect to the origin of life and all of its forms, and of humankind, scientific investigations in the realm of nature have led to considerable amounts of information. The overall mechanisms which are thus described are given the general name of evolution. Unfortunately, however, the word evolution does not always mean the same thing to all people using it and expressing viewpoints about it. Inconsistencies and a lack of common understanding of just what the word evolution means are frequently involved in debate within both scholarly and lay communities, on the interrelationships between information obtained from the Bible and from scientific investigation of the realm of nature. Let us take a closer look at the meaning of the term, by distinguishing between chemical and biological evolution and by noting some of the more significant aspects of each of them.

Chemical Evolution

The term chemical evolution refers to naturalistic concepts of how the first simple, primitive substances that were living in the sense of being self-reproducing may have developed from non-living substances. Scientific knowledge concerning chemical evolution is derived in large part from (a) best approximation about the chemical and physical forms which may have existed on earth prior to the appearance of life and about the environment in which they existed, and (b) laboratory experiments to ascertain chemical reactions which occur under those conditions. Some interesting results have been obtained, for example, the production of a few amino acids. It is obvious, however, that whatever results are obtained in (b) are determined by the assumptions made in (a), and there is considerable uncertainty about the validity of those assumptions. Furthermore, the substances produced in (b) fall far short of being living matter. For example, the amino acids produced in these experiments differ from those in living matter in their spatial structures and in their linkages one to another.

For these and other reasons, any conclusions from experimental attempts to study the postulated processes of chemical evolution must be considered to be very highly speculative. Furthermore, this type of investigation can reveal at best what might have occurred and not necessarily what did occur.

Biological Evolution

What do we mean by the term biological evolution? According to one study of relevant scientific writings, the term evolution is used in biological science in three ways: (a) change over time, (b) relationships of organisms by descent through common ancestry, and (c) a particular explanatory mechanism such as natural selection for the pattern and processes of (a) and (b). It is not unusual to find that the distinctions between these meanings are overlooked, even within the writings of a single author. The inevitable result of doing so is confusion and/or understanding for the writer and reader alike.

As we proceed in this section we will adopt a meaning essentially the same as that of (b) above. Thus, biological evolution refers to naturalistic concepts that all of the many kinds of plants and animals existing at the present time have descended from previously existing organisms by gradual modifications which have accumulated in successive generations.

Crucial to this general concept of biological evolution by common descent is the general mechanism which is generally attributed to it. This mechanism consists basically of the process of natural selection. This is the concept that any group of plants or animals tends to undergo variation, with more total organisms of each kind being produced than can obtain food and survive; so those individuals which possess characteristics which give them some advantage over other individuals in the competition for existence will most likely survive and the successful variations are transmitted to future generations. The mutations are generally very minute. Some of them may accumulate and lead to greater changes in the organisms involved. Mutations in fact have been induced artificially, for example by such processes as radiation with x-rays and with emanations from radioactive substances, by ultra-violet radiation, and even by chemical reagents. Natural selection on a relatively short time scale is illustrated by the rise of a "new" strain of mosquitoes or of flies after extended treatment with an insecticide that is quite effective in killing what had been the dominant strain. Whether these short term instances of evolution by natural selection can be extrapolated to grosser changes over longer time periods is a much more complex question.

Scientific evidences for the general concept of biological evolution come from many different types of investigation, full descriptions of which lie beyond the scope of this book. Nevertheless, we should consider in summary form what some major ones are. One type of evidence of evolution, interpreting this to indicate common ancestry, is found in observations that various types of biological entities exhibit structural similarities. For example, the forelimbs of several animal forms exhibit a five-digit bony structure, although to conclude that this necessarily means a common ancestry is to go beyond the observable evidence. Another lies in the existence of vestigial structures, that is, parts of organs which were well developed in ancestral forms but which no longer have any apparent function. For example, it was assumed up to recent decades that the human appendix is vestigial, and many people seem to get along quite well after its surgical removal. However, it is now quite evident that it is involved in a human immune function. Also some people get along quite well with a missing finger or arm, neither of which can be classed as being without function. Yet another line of evidence for biological evolution is found in the similarities in protein sequence which are found in various biological entities. It is well established that similarities do exist, but just how conclusive this evidence may be for common descent is a subject of conjecture.

Many different fields of scientific investigation are involved in these evidences. One of these is paleontology, which includes the finding, cataloging, and interpreting of the fossil record. Fossils consist not only of the actual bones and other hard components of earlier organisms, but also of impressions made by them as, for example, in mud which has hardened into rock and thus been preserved. A different, yet closely related type of evidence comes from that branch of geology which deals with rock strata. Sedimentary rocks are those which have been formed by the accumulation of sand and mud sediments at the bottoms of lakes, oceans, and so forth. Another contributing science is that of taxonomy, which is the science of naming, describing, and classifying organisms. Within or related to this broad field of investigation, relevant areas include comparative anatomy, comparative physiology and biochemistry, embryology, and genetics. Observations of the geographic distributions of plants and animals contribute to knowledge in this broad, general area.

How strong are the scientific evidences from these and other types of scientific investigation that the general concept of biological evolution is correct? Here it is only fair to recognize that this concept has been useful in scientific work. By scientifically useful we mean (a) that it has been effective in tying together many, many pieces of scientific knowledge and understanding and (b) that it has been successful as further experiments and observations are made in correlating many additional scientific observations and experimental results. To be sure the concepts of biological evolution have been refined and changed over the years and this is clearly an ongoing process, but this is characteristic of scientific explanation in other areas as well. On this basis alone, the concept of biological evolution has been and still is of considerable significance and value in science.

No broadly based scientific explanation is totally without weaknesses as well as strengths, and biological evolution is no exception in this regard. Here is a brief listing of some current weaknesses and limitations.

First, biological evolution is often claimed to be fact when in actuality it is generalized scientific explanation which is based on many scientific facts and which necessarily includes interpretations of those facts. As with other scientific explanation, it is a composite of many facts and interpretations. It may be equally misleading to refer to biological evolution as simply a theory, because that term could imply incorrectly that it is no more than a mere guess.

Second, only a very small fraction of the total time span which was presumably involved is available for study. Much of the scientific reasoning is extrapolation from observations of materials and processes existing within this limited time span. In science, we can indeed describe processes occurring now with good precision and accuracy, and those in the recent past with a reasonably high degree of confidence based on circumstantial evidences and knowledge of present processes. To be realistic, however, extrapolations to the more distant past are quite uncertain; both in interpreting circumstantial evidences over such long time periods and in ascertaining what the "experimental conditions" were like so long ago.

Third, there are imperfections in the fossil record. For example, many organisms apparently left no fossils; the record is deficient in the invertebrates; the record exhibits preferential bias to certain habitats. People who are advocates for the evolutionary viewpoint do not deny the incompleteness of the fossil record. Rather they explain it in ways which, no matter how rational they may be, really do nothing to make the record more complete.

Fourth, the evidences indicate that rather sudden, abrupt changes took place from time to time, but explanations for these occurrences are lacking. For example, the separations of time into the geological ages were apparently marked by abrupt happenings; the fossil record indicates that most changes were small ones of preexisting structures but that occasional new adaptive systems appeared quite suddenly. The change from the pre-Cambrian age to the Cambrian age is accompanied by the rather sudden appearance of well-developed animal fossils.

Fifth, the fossil evidence is frequently interpreted on the basis that prior existence and similarity in structure necessarily mean descent. This is nothing more nor less than an assumption, which is neither verifiable nor falsifiable by accepted scientific methods.

Sixth, some evidences from the cultural area are not entirely consistent with commonly accepted evolutionary development. For example, languages presumably evolved from the relatively simple to the relatively complex, but modern linguistic studies have revealed that even some of the most primitive cultures have extremely complex language structures.

Seventh, and this is especially important, there is even now very little progress in developing a quantitative theory of evolution. Scientific theories are generally accorded greater confidence if they are quantitative, not merely descriptive or qualitative, so that quantitative predictions of further experimental observations can be made and verified. No calculations have been made of the probabilities of the origins and developments occurring according to evolutionary processes, to verify whether there has been sufficient time for these mechanisms to have operated. It is not adequate merely to state that a "long time" was required and that a few billion years were available. Furthermore, some attempts which have been made in the direction of quantifying the concept of biological evolution have not turned out to be in full support of that concept.

None of these or other weaknesses or limitations in the scientific evidences definitively disprove the validity of the overall concept of biological evolution. However, they do collectively suggest that caution is in order in accepting what is claimed by many to be its unequivocal certainty.

There is often a tendency in science to maintain a particular scientific explanation which has been found to be useful, even if it does have weaknesses and limitations, unless or until a better alternative explanation arises. So, is there any scientific alternative to the concept of biological evolution? (Remember that we are considering here the how question and not the who question.) Two points should be made in response to this question. First, the validity of any theory must ultimately rise or fall on its own strengths and weaknesses, not on whether a better alternative explanation has been developed. A poor theory is not made valid simply because no one has proposed a better theory. Second, there can be proposed scientific alternatives to at least some crucial parts of the evolutionary concept. Consider the diagram,

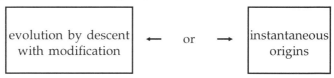

The left box represents the common evolutionary view. The right box represents, as an alternative, the concept that at several significant points (the exact number is unimportant) new forms of plant or animal life suddenly appeared on earth without descending from any form of prior existence on earth. Furthermore, a scientific, naturalistic mechanism can be postulated for the alternative in the right-box, namely, that the new forms of life arrived on earth by travel from some extraterrestrial source. This proposed mechanism is generally disregarded, and it should be, as far as scientific investigation is concerned, not because it has been proven to be incorrect but because it is not scientifically useful. That is to say, it is not scientifically testable. Yet it is only fair to point out that whether a proffered explanation of something which occurred in the distant past is either verifiable or falsifiable by the methods of modern science really has nothing to do with whether it really did happen that way.

We have used more space in dealing with the weaknesses than with the strengths of the evidences for biological evolution not because we wish to convey the impression that the weaknesses outweigh the strengths, but because in the teaching of science the concept of biological evolution frequently comes through as being much more definitive and final than it really is. There are limitations and unsolved problems in this area of science as in any other and to overlook their existence is inconsistent with the essence and the spirit of scientific investigation and explanation. Nevertheless, as indicated earlier, the overall concepts of biological evolution are based on many diverse types of scientific observation, and this concept has proven to be useful and effective in tying together many pieces of scientific knowledge and understanding and in predicting and correlating many ongoing, additional scientific observations and experimental results.

Relating Together Information from the Two Sources

Both the Bible and scientific investigation of nature are sources of information about the origins of the earth, the universe, life, and human beings. We have considered these two sources separately thus far in this chapter. How does the information obtained from one source relate to that from the other? Do they deal with different aspects of origins, or do they overlap in any way? And if they overlap, do they reenforce each other, or are they contradictory?

First, only the Bible addresses directly the who question and the why question, that is, the questions of who accomplished the origins and the purpose for which it was done. The Bible clearly and repeatedly indicates that God "created the heavens and the earth" and all that they contain. The results of the scientific investigation of nature do not indicate who did it, though human beings do at times find in nature support for their own divergent views about whether God did it and even about whether God exists. The Bible in various ways indicates something of God's purposes in his creative acts. Scientific data do not establish any particular purpose in nature, although they do at times lead to inconclusive and diverse speculation about whether there is any purpose in it.

The When Question

Both sources of information provide some information about when the origins took place. If the Genesis record is interpreted to mean that the six days of creation were six successive twenty-four-hour periods, then there is considerable disparity with the conclusion from scientific investigations that the origins of the items described in those six days were spread over a period of a few billion years or so. However, that interpretation of the meaning of day in Genesis 1 is surely not the only one which can be derived from the study of the Bible alone. Indeed, as we have noted, there are indications within the Bible itself that these days were very likely longer periods of time of indefinite duration. If the latter is the proper interpretation of the meaning of the days of creation, the differences between information obtained from the two sources tend to disappear. It is well to note, however, that there is no valid basis on which to quantify the meaning of the term "day" as it is used in the creation account.

We should recognize at this point that there are two additional, alternative interpretations of the Genesis record, both of which result in increasing the total time in Genesis 1 beyond six twenty-four-hour periods. One is to insert a long time-gap between Genesis 1:1 and 1:2. According to this interpretation, there was an original, perfect creation in Genesis 1:1 that was ruined during that time-gap and then was reconstructed beginning with 1:2. The other alternative interpretation is to equate each day with one thousand years so that an elapsed time of six thousand years was used in the total process. Without going into detail here, suffice it to say that both alternative interpretations are invalid, not because they disagree with scientific evidences (which they do) but because they are very inconsistent with the biblical language and with the context within the Bible in which these chapters are found.

We conclude, then, that information derived from the scientific investigation of nature about when the origins occurred adds to that derived from the Bible but does not contradict it, when considered from valid interpretations both of scientific data and of the Bible.

The How Question

In turning next to the how question of origins, we find that both the Bible and the scientific investigation of nature provide some information about what processes were involved. Of considerable basic significance is the recognition that both sources provide information that points to the conclusion that there were beginnings. The solar system and the earth did not always exist; they came into existence at some time in the past. There has not always been life on earth, and humankind has had a finite time of existence on earth.

A second point of basic significance is the recognition that both the Bible and scientific study in the realm of nature lead to the conclusion that there was an orderly progression and sequence in the appearances of the several components of nature. The sequence as described in the Bible in the first chapter of Genesis, assuming that the listed "days" followed each other in order, is light and darkness, separation of the earth as entity from the space surrounding it, land and water on the surface of the earth, vegetation on earth, cycles of days and seasons of years, water creatures and birds, land creatures, and man. The sequence as it is most commonly derived from scientific study of nature bears at least a rough similarity.

The scientific record is necessarily limited to mechanisms and means within the realm of nature and can deal only with matter and energy and their actions and interactions. To do differently would be inconsistent with the very essence of what science is. The Bible, if it is the inspired Word of God (as we are taking it to be), is neither limited to the realm of nature nor excluded from it because God is transcendent and immanent. So, in relating information obtained from the two sources to each other, we are really concerned with what the Bible indicates about natural mechanisms and processes in origins and with how whatever it does so indicate relates to information obtained from the scientific investigation of nature. In getting information from the Bible, we are, of course, limited to whatever the Bible says on it; we are interested in how God did what he did in creation and not in what he could have done differently.

The Bible really says very little about how God did what he did in this area. There are indications in the choice of language (create, make, form, for example) that he involved the use of ordinary natural processes and common natural materials already existing. There are indications in such terminology as "let the earth bring forth" that natural processes were used. While these and other specific wordings do not necessarily prove that he did make extensive use of such processes, they at least collectively tend more to corroborate than to contradict the information obtained from scientific investigation of nature — that such processes were involved in some of the very same stages of origins which are identified in the Genesis account.

We conclude, then, that there is some overlap of information about the processes of origins as obtained from the two sources, that much of this overlap is in agreement rather than contradictory, and that as of the present time much more of our knowledge in this area comes from the scientific study of nature than from the Bible.

Uniqueness of Being Human

As we have noted, the biblical record indicates in several ways that humans, while a part of creation, occupy a unique role in comparison to other parts of that which has been created. Humankind is described not merely as another plant or animal form which the earth brought forth, but as beings unique in essence — created in the image of God, and unique in role on earth — responsible for dominion or rule over the rest of creation. Whether we have wisely and effectively fulfilled the latter responsibility is not the issue here.

The scientific investigations of origins in nature result in descriptions of some characteristics of humans which are distinctive in comparison to other material beings. However, they really do not provide any basis for this uniqueness. Other forms of life have their own distinctive as well. If we humans are merely another stage in a long evolutionary process, there is really no basis for considering that we are to be particularly unique. Other forms of life have arisen and become extinct, so there is no reason to assume that humankind should be any different. In brief, then, information obtained both from the Bible and from scientific investigations in nature ascribe distinct uniqueness to humans, but only the Bible provides any basic explanation for it.

Why, Then, All the Controversy?

It appears, if the foregoing analyses of information on origins obtained from the study of the Bible and from the scientific study of nature are anywhere near correct, (a) that each source provides information that the other does not, and (b) that wherever the two sources overlap they are basically reenforcing rather than contradictory. Why, then, has there been so much controversy over these relationships? Let us now suggest and comment on possible reasons.

Much of the controversy has centered on this question — creation or evolution, take your pick. This is actually a false comparison, a pair of concepts which are not alternatives to each other. Thus, it is inevitable that controversy and differences of understanding should arise from this question. To get a rational answer, one must ask a rational question. The term creation necessarily signifies a creator, so this part is really a who question. The term evolution refers basically to naturalistic mechanisms, so this part is really a how question. Thus, the terms creation and evolution are not logical alternatives to each other.

Consider this diagram:

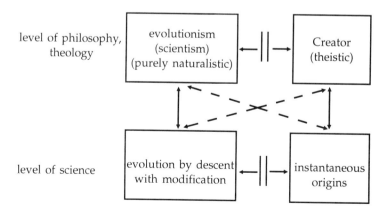

The lower half represents the level of science and the upper half the level of philosophy and theology. Within each of these two areas, science and philosophy/theology, there are many subtopics, one of which is that which deals with the origins of the numerous living forms which live on earth now or have done so in the past. Within this subtopic, the level of science deals primarily with (a) questions of "what," that is, with qualitative and quantitative descriptions of what these many living forms are, and (b) questions of how they all came into being as far as this can be described within the realm of nature. The level of philosophy/theology deals primarily with questions of who, also of why, and is not necessarily limited to the realm of nature in its concepts and explanations.

Two mutually exclusive alternatives are indicated in the boxes within the level of science. These are scientific alternative answers to how the many living forms originated on earth. This part of the diagram is the same as that shown and discussed on page 62.

Two mutually exclusive alternatives are indicated in the boxes within the level of philosophy and theology. The left one, evolutionism or scientism, represents the viewpoint that there is no valid source of knowledge other than science, that the only valid methodology in gaining knowledge is scientific methodology. The right-side box, creator, represents the viewpoint that there was or is a creator who accomplished the origins and who transcends that which was created, so is not entirely contained within the realm of nature. These two are mutually exclusive in that the one on the right is theistic while the one on the left is nontheistic or at least agnostic or pantheistic.

The problem in asking the question, creation or evolution is that "creation" deals with the upper-right box which is in the realm of philosophy and theology, while "evolution" deals with the lower-left box which is in the realm of nature and with naturalistic explanation.

This would merely be a problem of semantics if indeed the upper-left box necessarily signified the lower-left box as well, and if the two right-hand boxes necessarily went together. However, this definitely is not the case. On the one hand, the upper-left can combine with the lower-right as, for example, in our mention of the idea of extraterrestrial sources of new biological forms from time to time. On the other hand, the upper-right can combine with the lower-left as, for example, in the concept that God created by making use of ordinary natural processes throughout. Thus, either upper-box can combine with either lower-box, as indicated by the broken lines joining them.

The unfortunate consequence of this confusion is that many arguments which have purported to be over the alternatives on the level of science have in fact been arguments over the alternatives on the level of philosophy/theology. Frequently people who have basic commitment to the theistic position on the upper level have superimposed that commitment on the lower-right box and assumed they must intellectually or emotionally oppose the lower left box. At the same time many people who are committed to the validity of the lower-left box, on the level of science, have superimposed that commitment on the upper-left position and vigorously opposed the upper-right.

To be sure, there are problems with origins at the level of science, and there are significant and basic differences between the viewpoints at the upper level. But any argument over the basic differences between the purely naturalistic and theistic viewpoints of the upper level, carried on by superimposing it on the lower level, is simply not valid. To accept or to reject one or the other scientific views based on facts observable in nature and the scientific interpretations of them does not determine whether one must in consistency adopt either one of the philosophical views. The latter choice is ultimately one of faith and belief, not one of science per se. Likewise, to make commitment by faith to either the theistic or the purely naturalistic viewpoint on the upper-level does not dictate which of the scientific alternatives one must accept.

Another form in which controversy often appears in relating to each other the biblical and scientific sources of information regarding origins is the question of chance or design, one or the other. The issue of design in the realm of nature has long been a topic of considerable interest to many people. Even now it is the focus of considerable attention for many contemporary scholars. Observable evidences of design in nature are virtually unavoidable, but is this design apparent or real? Here we should exercise considerable caution for two reasons. First, it is not at all appropriate to rule design out completely based on observations in nature. Consider, for example, the observation of a pair of dice lying on a table and assume that the numbers 2 and 4 are on top — did these numbers come up by chance or by design of someone who put them that way? Unless we actually saw the roll or saw someone deliberately place the 2 and 4 on top, we cannot conclude definitely either way. Even in a larger scale study of natural objects or processes involving many repeated observations, we should be cautious in concluding that what is observed is strictly either by chance or by design, because overall statistical randomness is inherent in much of nature and thus can be considered in this sense to be part of the design built into nature.

Second, and probably of even more basic significance, the design vs. chance question is quite analogous to the creation vs. evolution question discussed above. The term chance can signify recognition only of natural processes and, if it extends at all to the philosophical level, implies a purely naturalistic, philosophical viewpoint. And the term design clearly does imply a designer. So the prior discussion of confusing philosophical/theological alternatives with scientific alternatives is applicable also to the chance vs. design question. Once again, to extrapolate from scientific evidences of apparent design or of apparent randomness to claim proof either of a theistic or a purely naturalistic basis of origins is to extrapolate beyond the realm of science into the realm of philosophy and theology, a topic to which we will return in chapter five.

There are unsolved problems in the scientific area of knowledge dealing with origins. The preponderance of viewpoint among many people is that the origins proceeded generally as indicated by the lower-left box in the figure above. However, the teaching of science is such that this viewpoint often comes through to students and thus to the public, probably to many scientists as well, as being much more definitive than it really is. There are limitations to science per se, and there are weaknesses in the sense of open questions and unsolved problems in scientific evolutionary theory. It is the author's observation that these qualifying factors are generally recognized more openly in textbooks dealing with advanced levels of scientific subject matter than in more elementary textbooks and explanations. Unfortunately most members of the public and many scientists specializing in other fields of science do not get to these more advanced texts. To be consistent with the essence of scientific explanation in general and evolutionary concepts in particular, these factors should receive more attention than they do. Nevertheless, the distinctions between the scientific and the philosophical/theological levels should be recognized. The status of the validity of the theistic viewpoint does not rise or fall based on whatever developments may come in the future relating to scientific study of the times and mechanisms of origins. To make this statement implies a form of faith and belief, another topic which will arise again in chapter five.

Chapter Four

What About Miracles?

The purposes of this chapter are twofold: to identify the meaning of the word miracle in referring to events which are described in the Bible, and to consider the who question and the how question, that is, who accomplished biblical miracles and how it was done.

Meaning of "Miracle"

An understanding of the meaning of the word miracle may be derived from an analysis of its use in the Bible, with due consideration both of the etymology of the word itself and the contexts in which it is used. The word miracle occurs in its singular or plural form thirty-seven times in the Bible. (The word-study in this section is based on the text of the King James version.) Five of these uses are in the Old Testament and are translations from three different Hebrew words. One of these Hebrew words is *mopheth*, which is found in Exodus 7:9 and Deuteronomy 29:3, and comes from a root meaning conspicuous; this word means miracle in the sense of something so conspicuous and unusual that it arouses wonder by those who observe it or learn of it. Another of the Hebrew words is *pala*, in Judges 6:13, which signifies an accomplishment which is hard — a concept which ties in closely with the characteristic of being conspicuous and unusual. The third Hebrew word which is translated into English as miracle is *owth*; it is in Numbers 14:22 and Deuteronomy 11:3 and signifies something which is a flag or a beacon, that is, a sign or token of something other than itself.

The thirty-two appearances of the word miracle in the New Testament are translations from two different Greek words. One is *dunamis*, which comes from a root meaning power or force; it means miracle in the sense of a mighty, powerful work — a concept not unlike that emphasized by the Hebrew *mopheth* and *pala*. The other Greek word translated into the same English word is *semelon*, which signifies a sign or a token; this concept is essentially the same as that of the Hebrew *owth*. Nearly one-third of the New Testament usages are from *dunamis* and slightly over two-thirds from *semelon*.

This brief study of the origins of the word miracle as it appears in the Bible indicates that a miracle is an event which is characterized by two features: (1) it is extraordinary and unusual, in that it stands out as conspicuous, it is mighty and powerful, and it arouses wonder; and (2) it is not something which is complete or self-contained, but is a sign or token of something beyond itself.

The context in which the word miracle appears can contribute to further understanding of its meaning. All five of the Old Testament uses of miracle, singular or plural, refer to events relating to the departure of the people of Israel from Egypt, sometime around 1400 B.C. One of these references, Exodus 7:9, refers specifically to something which Aaron did before Pharaoh prior to that departure, namely to the throwing down of his rod which then became a serpent. The other four Old Testament references apply more generally to a longer series of events, all of which are attributed to God and occurred prior to and during the flight from Egypt.

In the New Testament, the contexts in which the word miracle appears explain who accomplished the events to which it refers. In some instances, it was Jesus during the time of his public ministry on earth. In others, it was one of the apostles, such as Stephen, Philip, Barnabas, or Paul. When the action was performed by an apostle, the power and the authority for doing it is attributed to God. Some of these New Testament references are to specific events and others more generally to groups of events. In brief, a study of the contexts within which the word miracle appears corroborates the validity of the two characteristics of its meaning which were derived from an analysis of the Hebrew and Greek words, and they add a third characteristic — the miracles were performed by God, either directly or through a prophet or an apostle.

The three characteristics of the meaning of miracle may be combined to form a working definition: *a miracle is an extraordinary event which is accomplished by God as a sign of some purpose of his own.* This definition is essentially the same as one found in Webster's dictionary. Thus, a miracle is a historical event; it involves material objects, people, or other physical entities; it is observable by people through one or more of their five natural senses; it is something accomplished by God, either by acting directly or by his power acting through a prophet or apostle; it is something which is done for God's purpose — not merely something of no significance or consequence.

The word miracle is sometimes used in everyday conversation in its biblical sense. Nevertheless, it is often used differently in senses which differ from biblical usage in either one or both of two ways. First, the term is often used with no recognition of God as the one who accomplishes it. Second, and not necessarily in combination with the first, it is often used about things which occur frequently and/or for which natural mechanisms and causes are either known or assumed to exist. For example, in modern everyday terminology, life itself may be called a miracle. Or a miracle may be something which arouses human emotions of wonder and awe, as when one views a sunset, the vastness of space, the marvels of the human eye, or a vista in the Rocky Mountain National Park. Or it may be something that accomplishes a desired goal, such as a "miracle drug" for treating an infection or a "miracle detergent" for use in the family's washing machine. Or it may merely be some phenomenon which one cannot explain or does not understand, as the working of a television set by anyone who is not a technical expert in electronics and electromagnetic radiation, the driving of an automobile by someone who has no idea at all of what really goes on in the motor,

74

or the contemplation of the transport of a functioning instrumented laboratory to the surface of Mars. Or it may be acts of Providence, such as the self-healing capability of the human body or the coming of rain after a time of drought, whether these phenomena are attributed to the power of God or not.

Miracles in the Bible

The descriptions of miracles in the Bible are not limited to events which are identified by use of the word. Some of the same events are described or referred to in two or more places in the Bible, both with and without use of the term miracle. Other events are described which meet the same three criteria so can be classified as miracles. A study of all such events enables one to obtain further knowledge about the miracles of the Bible.

When Miracles Were Accomplished

Miracles are concentrated particularly in three parts of the historical times covered by the Old and New Testaments. The first of these is during the times of Moses and Joshua. During this period, which was centered around 1400 B.C., Moses was established as a leader, the people of Israel were enabled to leave Egypt, they survived for several decades in desert regions, and they were reestablished as a nation with their own homeland.

The second period of miracles is during the times of the prophets Elijah and Elisha, centering around 850 B.C. During this period, the nation of Israel, which was then functioning as a kingdom or, more precisely, as two kingdoms, was deeply engulfed in a struggle with idolatry.

The third period in which miracles were concentrated is during the first century A.D. This period began with the birth of Christ, continued through his public ministry, and ended with the establishment and growth of the early Christian church.

Some miracles took place at other times, including among others the time of the prophet Daniel. However, most miracles which are described as historical events in the Bible are concentrated in these three periods.

Types of Miracles

The miracles of the Bible vary so much one from another that it is difficult to classify them into a few categories. Those occurring in the times of Moses and Joshua included some involving mastery over natural objects and forces on a grand scale, such as the parting of the Red Sea and the observable presence of a cloud to give traveling direction to the Israelites by day and a pillar of fire by night. Others involved individual material objects on a smaller scale as, for example, the rod which interchangeably became a serpent, or the bush which was aflame but was not consumed. Some miracles were directed toward one or a few observers, such as the burning bush which was for Moses' own benefit; others were directed toward larger numbers of direct beneficiaries, such as the provision for the Israelites of water from a rock or the inflicting of the plagues on the people of Egypt. Some miracles were directed toward the giving of emphasis to spiritual information, as the scenes from the mountain top which accompanied the giving of the Ten Commandments to Moses; others were directed toward the meeting of physical needs, as was the provision of manna and quail for the people of Israel during their sojourn in the desert.

The miracles during the times of Elijah and Elisha likewise were of various types. One miracle or group of miracles, described in 1 Kings 19, involves common forces of nature such as wind, earthquake, and fire, but with uncommon circumstances and significance. Others involved the provision of food under circumstances such that they must be described as miracles. Another miracle, the termination of Elijah's life on earth, was surely unique in comparison to other deaths before and since that time.

During the few years of Christ's public ministry, he performed many miracles. According to one analysis of the biblical record, seventeen involved bodily cures, nine consisted of exercising control over environmental forces of nature, six resulted in the curing of demoniacs, and three involved raising individuals to life who were dead. An analysis like this cannot be either complete or precise, because of the arbitrary form of these or any other categories and, especially, because the Bible refers generally to many more miracles which Christ performed but which are not identified individually.

The birth and death of Christ were accompanied by miracles of still different types. He was born of the Virgin Mary, and the time of his birth was accompanied by the angelic announcement and by the star which then led the Wise Men to where he was. His death by crucifixion was accompanied by observable events which can properly be classed as miracles, such as the darkness during daytime and the rending of the temple veil. It was followed on the third day by what some have called the greatest miracle of all, the resurrection.

The early years of the Christian church, as described in the book of Acts and in some of the New Testament epistles, saw many more miracles accomplished by or through the apostles. Some involved physical healings. Others involved the speaking of languages which were not normal to the speakers but which were known and understood by the listeners.

Purposes of Miracles

While there is little commonality in type of miracles in the Bible, there is much in common among their purposes. One major purpose, perhaps the most frequently significant one, is to authenticate the mission of God or of his chosen prophet or apostle in dealing with his people. One Old Testament example is described in Exodus 4 — the purpose of the changing of Moses' rod into a serpent and back again was to be a sign to Pharaoh (and to Moses and Aaron themselves) that it was God's mission that they were undertaking. A New Testament statement of the same general purpose of miracles is given in

2 Corinthians 12:12, "The signs of a true apostle were performed among you with all perseverance, by signs and wonders and miracles."

There were both immediate and longer range purposes of some miracles. For example, the parting of the Red Sea was for the obvious immediate purpose of enabling the Israelites to pass through to the other side and thus to escape from the Egyptians who were pursuing them. In addition there was a more basic purpose, which was to demonstrate to the Israelites the power of God and his control over them at that early, crucial stage of their flight from Egypt.

The basic purpose of miracles is to show God's involvement, and extends not only to people who directly observed the events but also to people who subsequently read of them in the inspired writings of the Bible. This principle is stated, for example, in John 20:31, "but these (that is, those miracles of Jesus which are recorded in the preceding verses and chapters) have been written that you may believe that Jesus is the Christ, the Son of God; and that by believing you may have life in His name."

Many miracles performed by Jesus, such as the healing of the sick, fulfilled the additional purpose of expressing his sympathy for suffering humanity. Surely he was very sympathetic with individual people who suffered, empathizing with their needs and feelings. Several times he gave specific commands to his followers to have this same sensitivity and to act on it. By performing miracles of healing, he reinforced these commands by his own example. Yet this purpose of miracles must be understood in the context that he performed such miracles only in selected cases.

Limitation to Selected Cases

The use of miracles throughout the historical times of the Bible was limited to special cases. To be sure, we do not know all the specific miracles which were accomplished, as is emphasized, for example, in John 20:30, "Many other signs therefore Jesus also performed in the presence of the disciples, which are not written in this book." Nevertheless, it is abundantly clear that not all of the sick people were healed by Jesus or by the apostles in the early church; one who was not healed is even identified by name in 2 Timothy 4:20, "but Trophimus I left sick at Miletus." During the period described in the book of Acts, when many miracles were being accomplished, miracles are mentioned in only about one-half of the cities in which the work of the apostles is described. Of all the deaths which must have occurred during Jesus' three-year public ministry, to the best of our knowledge he raised only three of them back to life — a daughter of Jairus, the son of a widow of Nain, and Lazarus; and presumably all three of those died subsequently.

Therefore, we conclude that the miracles of the Bible were concentrated within certain historical periods, and that even in those periods they were done only in selected cases. This is not to say that God is himself subject to any limitations in his miracle-working power. It is to say that God, for his own purposes, does not always choose to demonstrate his power in this way.

How Miracles Were Accomplished

We noted in our consideration of the meaning of the word miracle that all miracles were accomplished by God, either directly or through a prophet or an apostle. The answer to the who question about miracles is clearly that God did it. To raise now the how question, about how the miracles were accomplished, does not in any way rule out or even call into question the concept that God did it.

We must rely heavily on the Bible itself for information about how the biblical miracles were accomplished, simply because the miracles are in their very essence unique events. At the same time we should recognize that these miracles were events which occurred in the realm of nature, involved material objects or natural forces, and were observable at the time to one or more human beings through their natural senses. It may thus appear that we could probably obtain added information about how the miracles were accomplished from other sources of knowledge concerning nature. This indeed may be the case, but only in a limited sense because the miracles were unique events rather than events which are repeatable and thus amenable to scientific investigation now.

Sometimes the biblical discussion of a particular miracle indicates that some natural process or mechanism was involved in it. Consider, for example, the parting of the Red Sea. It is indicated in Exodus 14:21 not only that God did it but also something about how he did it: "and the Lord swept the sea back by a strong east wind all night, and turned the sea into dry land, so the waters were divided." Thus, a part of the explanation about how the waters were parted is that it was achieved by means of a strong east wind blowing all night. Were this factor not of some significance, it seems unlikely that the inspired writer would have bothered mentioning it. This is, of course, only a partial answer to the how question — we would presumably be safe in assuming that the wind has often blown in the same place, even from the east and even for all night, without resulting in the formation of a path of dry land through the body of water. If this were an everyday consequence of an everyday phenomenon, by definition it would not even be a miracle. Nevertheless, the fact remains that the biblical record of this and some other miracles includes specific mention of some natural processes which were involved in accomplishing it.

Even where the Bible does not mention any natural process or mechanism with a miracle, we should be very cautious about ruling out such a possibility. By way of a roundabout illustration, let us consider a particular experiment which I sometimes conducted as a lecture-demonstration before chemistry students. In this demonstration, a handkerchief is borrowed from a student in the class. This handkerchief is rinsed in a beaker which presumably contains water ("to wash it and make it clean before proceeding with the experiment"). It is then held by a pair of tongs and gently wafted near the flame of a Bunsen burner ("to dry it out more quickly"). But it catches on fire "accidentally" (but really on purpose), whereon it burns vigorously with a flame visible to the entire class ("Oh, I am so sorry, your handkerchief caught on fire"). After burning for a time, the flame is extinguished and the handkerchief returned to its owner — absolutely unburned and uncharred, and in its original condition except that it is now damp. Thus, the handkerchief has burned but has not been consumed. The "secret" of this experiment is that the beaker contained a mixture of methanol and water, not pure water. Thus, when ignited, the methanol burned off but the handkerchief itself was in fact soaking wet with water and could not burn at all.

This illustration brings to mind the biblical story of the bush which Moses saw burning with fire without being consumed, Exodus 3:2, "And the angel of the Lord appeared to him in a blazing fire from the midst of a bush, and he looked, and behold, the bush was burning with fire, yet the bush was not consumed." We are not claiming here that this particular bush had been soaked with a mixture of methanol and water and then ignited prior to the moment that Moses first observed it, although if that had happened Moses would have seen just what the biblical account said he did see. But we are suggesting here that we should be very hesitant to rule out the possibility that a natural process or mechanism may have been involved in a miracle simply because the Bible provides no information about the means by which it was accomplished. Many of the descriptions of miracles in the Bible are given with no indication of how they were done.

It might seem that we should be able to conduct experiments today to check out the biblical miracles. Presumably if we could do this we could obtain further information about how it was accomplished, or even to see if it really did come out as the biblical record indicates that it did. However, this really is not possible. Consider, for example, the miracle by which water was changed into wine at a wedding reception in the city of Cana. We could attempt to reconstruct this event experimentally by assembling a few large earthenware crocks, pouring water into them, and then withdrawing portions of the liquid for examination to determine whether it indeed is water or wine. Assuming for now that this examination revealed that the liquid was still water, what could we conclude from this experiment? We could conclude that, if the conditions in Cana were the same as in our experiment now, it was water and not wine that came out of the jars. We could then vary the experimental conditions with, for example, different prior treatments or uses of the crocks and with "water" from other sources and with alternative compositions. However, we simply do not know enough about the "experimental" conditions which existed in Cana to be able to reproduce them with any measure of completeness or exactness. Furthermore, we do know of one condition that we are decidedly unable to reproduce — the one who conducted this action in Cana was Jesus, who was, according to the full context of the biblical record, the incarnate God himself.

It is interesting to speculate about what additional types of evidence might have been preserved concerning this particular miracle. We might wish that a few sample vials of the final liquid had been preserved so that we could subject them to chemical analysis to provide further information about the how question for this miracle. However, even if this had been done, it is very unlikely that it could provide any meaningful information, either to prove or to supplement the biblical record. There would inevitably be contamination of the samples, deterioration by chemical or biological action over periods of time, etc.; and surely some prior generation would have used them up long before our time!

The biblical record of this miracle at Cana not only states that it did happen, but it also mentions some evidences which substantiate that statement. In particular, it refers to the reactions and responses of people who drank this liquid; these responses surely testify in support of the statement that the beverage which was taken out of the jars was different from the water which was put into them.

In brief, therefore, our scientific knowledge of phenomena in the realm of nature indicates that things do not usually happen the way the Bible says they did in Cana. The biblical record does not contradict that general situation, but presents this event as a unique one, which was accomplished by the incarnate God and was recognized by people at the time as unique. Furthermore, the biblical record of this miracle is consistent within itself in that the evidences which are described as resulting from the event are entirely consistent with what the event is stated to have been.

Finally, in this brief consideration of the how question concerning miracles described in the Bible, we are brought again to the recognition that the God of the Bible is both immanent within nature and transcendent to nature. In accomplishing miracles for his own purposes, he sometimes used his immanence, as in the blowing of the east wind in the parting of the waters of the Red Sea, and he sometimes used his transcendence, as in the incarnation itself and in the resurrection of Christ.

The Natural and the Supernatural

It is appropriate to include within this chapter, some summary comments on the concepts of the natural and the supernatural. In chapter three, we described nature as the realm of matter and energy, of the fundamental particles, and of the laws which describe their actions and interactions. This is the realm which is searchable, observable, and describable by the methods of scientific investigation.

There is a tendency to assume (as some primitive cultures do) either that God is nature or that God's activity is limited to readily observable natural phenomena, such as rain or drought, thunder and lightning, earthquakes, and volcanoes. In more advanced cultures which possess highly developed knowledge of the realm of nature, there is a tendency to assume that God exists, if at all, either apart from the realm of nature or in whatever residual gaps may exist at any particular time in the scientific knowledge and understanding of the realm of nature. Neither of these tendencies is consistent with what the Bible teaches concerning God and nature.

The first of two basic biblical factors in the relationships between God and nature is that God is the Creator of all that comprises the realm of nature. God is the Creator, and nature is created. This fundamental concept is stated, for example, in the Old Testament in Genesis 1:1, "In the beginning God created the heavens and the earth," and in the New Testament in Colossians 1:16, "For in Him all things were created, both in the heavens and on earth, visible and invisible, whether thrones or dominions or rulers or authorities — all things have been created through Him and for Him." However, the conclusion that God is the Creator of the realm of nature is not based on any one or few isolated statements in the Bible. Rather, it is a basic theme which permeates the content of the Bible, both directly and indirectly. No matter what one's view may be about the processes or mechanisms which were involved in these creative acts, and no matter what one's interpretation may be of biblical views on the "how questions," there can be no real doubt that the Bible teaches clearly that God is the Creator and that nature is created.

The second of two basic biblical factors in the relationships between God and nature is that God is also the Sustainer of the realm of nature. This concept, as the preceding one, is based on the overall thrust of the content of the Bible and not on the interpretation of any one or few isolated statements. However, references to certain biblical statements can serve to elaborate on the meaning of this basic concept. One passage which particularly emphasizes the point that God sustains that which he created is in Acts 17:24, 25, and 28, "The God who made the world and all things in it, since *He is Lord of heaven and earth,* does not dwell in temples made with hands, neither is He served by human hands, as though He needed anything, since *He Himself gives to all life and breath and all things ... in Him we live and move and exist ...* " (italics added). Another is in Colossians 1:17, "And He is before (i.e., has existed prior to) all things, and in Him all things hold together." That God's role as Sustainer is an all encompassing one is evident from the preceding verse, Colossians 1:16, from which it may be noted that the "all things" which are held together in God include the "heavens and the earth" and human events within that realm, "thrones or dominions or rulers or authorities."

Thus, the realm of nature is neither synonymous with God nor independent of him. God is the Creator of the realm of nature and also the Sustainer of that which he created. Therefore, God is the author of natural laws, which are derived from scientific investigations of nature to describe relationships and interrelationships within the realm of matter and energy, both in an ultimate sense (Creator/created) and in an ongoing sense (Sustainer/sustained). Natural laws are nothing more or less than explanations or descriptions of God's regular activity in sustaining that which he created. It is important that we emphasize at this point that it is fully possible for rational, intelligent human beings to study and to gain valid knowledge in the area of natural law without recognizing or believing that God did it and that God does it. In general, one can study many what questions and how questions ranging, for example, from the composition and functioning of a watch to the germination and growth of plants, without any knowledge or even interest in who designed the watch or the plants to have their particular structures and functions. At the same time it is equally important that we emphasize that one who accepts the biblical answer to the who questions relating to natural law does not for that reason have any automatic "inside" source of information about the structures and functions of natural objects within the realm of nature.

Let us turn now from the concept of the natural to that of the supernatural. It has been a common experience of many people in many cultures to believe that there exists a realm apart from the natural realm. This belief often takes the form of the occult, a term which basically means secret or mysterious and generally refers to knowledge or activity which is supernatural in the sense that it is not bounded by strict laws of modern science. One common form of the occult is that of astrology, which deals with natural objects and is presumed to involve natural cause-and-effect relationships which are of an unknown essence. Astrology, if indeed it does deal with the supernatural, does so only if the term supernatural is used to describe gaps in present scientific understanding. Another form of the occult is necromancy or magic, singly or in combination (or which may at times be nothing more than imagination exercised in the pursuit of fun). These and other forms of the occult are very common, not only in primitive cultures but also in the midst of cultures which are more advanced scientifically and in sophistication.

None of these forms of the occult are in any sense or to any degree synonymous with the meaning of the term supernatural when used in reference to the God of the Bible. In fact, the Bible recognizes the existence of the occult as something which is distinctly apart from God and his own workings. For example, the ability of "magicians" to engage in the practice of their "secret arts" to give the outer appearance of accomplishing feats like the extraordinary events caused by God is recognized in Exodus 7:11, "Then Pharaoh also called for the wisemen and the sorcerers, and they also, *the magicians of Egypt, did the same with their secret arts* making frogs come up on the land of Egypt." (italics added).

With respect to God's own actions, the Bible recognizes that God can act outside known natural laws. This is, in a sense, what is done in biblical miracles which, as described earlier in this chapter, are extraordinary events accomplished by God as signs of some purposes of his own. Such events involve natural objects or phenomena, are observable by one or more human beings through their natural senses, and must be unusual and different from the way things usually work out in nature. However, we would do well to avoid drawing sharp distinctions between the natural and the supernatural. Wellmeaning attempts to do so typically identify God with the supernatural and consider him to be apart from or irrelevant to the natural. This is surely not consistent with the biblical view that God is both Creator and Sustainer of the entire realm of nature.

Other well-meaning attempts to distinguish between the natural and the supernatural do so by equating the term natural with the way things usually function and behave, and the supernatural with unusual departures from what is the usual in nature. This is hardly consistent with some purely naturalistic observations. For example, it is not a frequent, everyday occurrence for the sun to be eclipsed by the moon, but complete physical cause-and-effect relationships can be identified and are well known to explain this rare occurrence (at least, rare within the everyday time references of human beings).

What, then is the meaning of the term supernatural? A dictionary definition of supernatural is "of, belonging to, having reference to, or proceeding from an order of existence beyond the physical universe that is observable and capable of being experienced by ordinary means; transcending nature in degree and in kind or concerned with what transcends nature." Taking this definition quite literally, we may note that (a) God himself is supernatural, (b) God can perform supernatural acts and in fact has done so as, for example, in the initial creation of matter and energy and in the incarnation and resurrection of Christ, (c) there is no sharp dividing line between the natural and supernatural because we never have complete, accurate knowledge of the "order of existence" which is "the physical universe." Therefore, we can hardly divide sharply between what does and what does not "transcend nature."

Besides this definition of the supernatural, there are ways of looking at nature other than that of scientific investigation, particularly those involving ethical and moral considerations and value judgments. Whether or not these fall into either the natural or supernatural categories, they are very much part of the biblical view of the relationships between God and nature.

The Bible itself does not draw sharp distinctions between the natural and the supernatural. In fact, the word supernatural does not even appear in the Bible (either New American Standard Bible or King James translation). However, the Bible records events which are to be recognized by faith as acts of God and are outside known and normal natural law. These are always done as signs for some purpose of God, John 4:48, "Jesus therefore said to him, 'Unless you people see signs and wonders, you simply will not believe,'" and Acts 2:19 (which is quoted from the Old Testament book of Joel), "And I will grant wonders in the sky above, and signs on the earth beneath, blood, and fire, and vapor of smoke." Furthermore, the Bible teaches that God is both transcendent to nature and immanent within nature, and that the same sovereign God who assures normal regularity within nature is not limited to that normal regularity in every thing that he does.

Chapter Five
Fitting It All Together

The preceding chapters have consisted primarily of analysis. We have attempted to analyze each topic by separating it into its component parts and then looking separately at each part. This particular method of analysis was outlined in chapter one by separating the questions: who, what, how, and why from each other, and by separating our sources of information into two categories: the study of the Bible and the scientific investigation of the realm of nature. This method of analysis was applied to a variety of historical events in chapter two, to the area of origins in chapter three, and to the topic of miracles in chapter four.

This chapter will consist primarily of synthesis. By this we mean the fitting together of the several component parts on some sort of coherent framework. This has been done to a limited extent in some of the preceding chapters, but we wish to do so now in the broader context of total world and life views.

The Concept of An Overall World View

One recurring characteristic of human beings throughout the ages of recorded history has been the questioning of one's own identity as an individual and the identity of humankind generally in the context of all reality and all meaning — Who am I? Where did humankind come from? What is my destiny? What is life all about? This questioning is expressed within a theistic framework of thought in Psalm 8:4, "What is man, that Thou dost take thought of him?" The same questioning is still deeply within the consciousness of people today, whether it be formulated within a theistic frame of reference or not. Knowledge and perceptions of knowledge obtained from the scientific investigation of nature are deeply involved in this questioning.

The German word *Weltanschauung* refers to a comprehensive conception or apprehension of the world as a whole. It refers to an overall view of the world: a world which includes all things and all events in it; past, present, and future time periods; and the purpose and the outlook for the world to the extent that they exist or are perceived to exist. A *Weltanschauung* includes views of all of life in the total context and environment of all other being and time in which life exists.

A direct translation of *Weltanschauung* into English results simply in the term *world view.* However, the word world is frequently used in everyday thought and communication in a more limited context, such as with reference to the physical realm or in contrast to the spiritual realm. Unfortunately there is no other well-established English word or phrase to represent *Weltanschauung,* and many English dictionaries list the German word itself. The term *world view,* as it is used in this chapter, represents the broader, more comprehensive concept of *Weltanschauung.*

The formulation of world views has been of considerable concern to philosophers, theologians, and other reasoning and reflecting people throughout all of recorded history. This is not merely an idle and harmless activity for those who have nothing better to do with their time and intellectual energy. Quite to the contrary, the world view held by an individual or group is very influential in determining behavior, as well as motivations, attitudes, and actions toward themselves, one another, and other factors external to themselves. Basic questions about a person's own identity and relationship to reality are philosophical questions that involve the presuppositions of world views.

Many views have been formulated and followed by human beings. Some are limited in scope while others are much more comprehensive. Some have been well thought out and formulated with considerable preciseness, while others are vague and ill-defined, even by the people who embrace them. Some views are based on reason, others on emotion, and most on some combination of both.

Any attempt to classify thought-systems as comprehensive as world views is inevitably going to suffer from the inadequacies of oversimplification. Nevertheless, some general comments in this direction may be appropriate in this introductory portion of this chapter.

Certain kinds of topics frequently recur and are discernible in various world views. The three chief ones are the basic concepts of humankind, nature, and a supreme being. Among these three kinds of concepts, one is often taken to be the primary, central one, although not necessarily to the exclusion of the other two. On this basis, world views can be classified into three groups — humanistic, naturalistic, or theistic — depending on whether the central and primary concept is, respectively, humankind, nature, or a supreme being.

In trying to apply this system of classification of world views, we discern two conflicting tendencies. One is for each topic to become exclusive of the others. For example, naturalism as a well-formulated philosophical system tends to stress the primacy of nature so completely that it rejects the concept of a supreme being. The other tendency is for a system to designate one concept as primary while retaining one or both of the other concepts in subsidiary and dependent status. Thus, for example, naturalism can include a concept of human beings strictly and solely as a part of nature. As further examples, some forms of humanism and naturalism can include a concept of a supreme being who consists of nothing more than human beings or nature, and a theistic system usually includes roles for human beings and nature that may be very significant though secondary to, and dependent on, the still higher concept of a supreme being.

There are variations and combinations of the categories within this simple classification. A few will be mentioned here, with no effort being made for completeness. Materialism, the system or doctrine that all things are basically material, is essentially a naturalistic view that tends to deny that there is any distinctiveness of life and what it is to be human apart from purely naturalistic considerations. Rationalism is the theory that the only valid means of obtaining knowledge is reason or, more specifically, the processes of logic and deduction. Thus, rationalism can include significant components of humanism, naturalism, or theism, although none of them need be exclusively or even primarily rationalism. Empiricism, as a formal philosophical system, is the theory that all knowledge comes from experience, a concept very different from that of rationalism. We will refer to these concepts further as we proceed through this chapter.

Scientism, Biblicism, and Christianity

The accompanying diagram is intended for reference throughout this section. As indicated to the left, the top third represents the area of world views, the middle third the area of systematized knowledge, and the lowest third the area of sources of the information which serves as "input data" for the systematic formulation of knowledge.

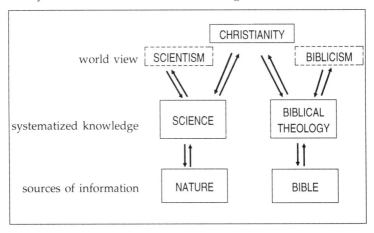

The two sources of information shown in the diagram are the ones described in chapter one. Nature is the realm of matter and energy and the fundamental laws which describe the actions, reactions, and interactions of matter and energy. The Bible consists of the written books of the Old and New Testament, the canonicity of which is reasonably well established as is also the content of the original manuscripts even though the latter have not been known to exist physically for many centuries.

One of the two bodies of systematized knowledge shown in the diagram, science, has been described in various contexts in the preceding chapters. The other one, biblical theology, merits further description here although the word theology was used without definition in chapter one. The word theology comes from two Greek words, *theos* and *logos,* which mean, respectively, God and word or rational discourse. The meaning is similar even today, for theology signifies the rational study of God, particularly in the interrelationships between God and human beings. Thus, a common dictionary definition states that theology is "the study of God and His relation to man and the world." Any area of systematized knowledge must have some source of input data or information on which the body of knowledge is built. The box in the diagram representing knowledge obtained from the Bible is labeled biblical theology, which is defined in the dictionary as the "theology that seeks to derive its categories of thoughts and the norms for its interpretations from the study of the Bible as a whole." Note in this definition that it is the Bible as a whole that (a) determines the subject matter of biblical theology ("categories of thoughts") and (b) is the standard of authority within biblical theology ("norms for its interpretations").

It is conceivable that other sources could be used for the information which is systematized to form a theology. For example, "natural theology" is defined in the dictionary as "theology deriving its knowledge of God from the study of nature independent of special revelation."

The methodologies of science and biblical theology are essentially very similar as was noted in chapter one, so much so that theology has often been called the "queen of the sciences." The practice of both is a human activity. Both involve interpreting that which is observable, assembling and classifying observations, "model-building" by formulating frameworks to tie various observations together and to explain them, and predicting further observations to test and to refine these explanations. These "models" and generalized explanations are derived by human beings, both in science and biblical theology, but they must be based on the input data obtained from their respective sources of information. The double arrows, between science and nature and biblical theology and the Bible, show the constant interplay back and forth between the areas of systematized knowledge and the sources of input data on which the knowledge is built.

Scientific explanations and biblical theological explanations are legitimately subject to challenge and modification, not from whim or fancy, or likes or dislikes, but because of their appeal to their respective sources of information. The authority in science consists of that which is there in nature, and the authority in biblical theology consists of that which is there in the Bible.

Scientism

Three types of world views are shown in the diagram. One of these is scientism, which is defined in the dictionary as "a thesis that the methods of the natural sciences should be used in all areas of investigation including philosophy, the humanities and the social sciences; a belief that only such methods can fruitfully be used in the pursuit of knowledge." The particular word scientism is not overly important, but the concept it represents is very significant. Note that scientism is a world view in the sense that it designates "all areas of investigation" and the "only … methods … in the pursuit of knowledge." It is an ideology and, like other ideologies, tends to be systematic and authoritarian and to be held tenaciously.

It should be made very clear that science is not scientism and that scientism is not science. Science is limited to the realm of nature, that is, to the realm of matter and energy, without specifying in any way what other realms may or may not exist. Scientism affirms that there is no other realm, that the ultimate reality waiting to be uncovered is material, and that there is no valid knowledge other than scientific knowledge. As someone has described it, scientism divides all thought into two categories, scientific knowledge and nonsense.

Some scientists subscribe to scientism as their own world view and ideology, while many others do not. Similarly some people, who are not scientists, subscribe to scientism while others do not. There is no necessary connection between a person as a scientist and his or her holding of scientism or any other particular world view.

Biblicism

Another type of world view shown in our diagram is biblicism, which is defined in the dictionary as "narrow or exclusive use of the Bible." As a world view, biblicism may be described as the view that biblical knowledge is valid but purely scientific knowledge is not. Just as scientism in effect rejects all knowledge except scientific knowledge, so biblicism accepts only that knowledge which is obtained from the Bible. Again, the particular word is not overly important, but the concept which biblicism represents is important.

Christianity

The third world view represented in the diagram is Christianity. This word, like so many others in common usage, does not always bear the same meaning, sometimes not even to two people who use it in trying to communicate with each other. To some, Christianity almost seems to be equated with theism — "I am not an atheist, so that makes me Christian, does it not?" To others, Christianity seems to be equated with a particular culture, or with advanced civilized cultures in general. Even when attempting to define or describe Christianity within a biblical context, some people equate Christianity with the exercising of faith and worship. However, none of these is an adequate concept of what Christianity is, so just what is it? *Christianity is the complete world view which is based on the God of the Bible as its primary fact.* As a total world view, Christianity includes the concepts of humankind and of the realm of nature. These are very high concepts and very significant ones, but they are secondary and dependent in comparison to God who is primary, independent, and sovereign.

With reference again to our diagram, Christianity as a total world view accepts both science and biblical theology as legitimate bodies of systematized knowledge, in full recognition of course of the essential features of what they both are. Furthermore, Christianity as a total world view includes both nature and the Bible as valid sources of input data and information, again in full recognition that the authority lies within these areas and not necessarily in any particular interpretation of them. The God of the Bible is both transcendent and immanent, permeating the entirety of nature and the Bible, but transcending beyond them — neither wholly contained in them nor limited to them.

The primacy of God is indicated, for example, in the first five words of the Bible, Genesis 1:1, "In the beginning God created … " God is primary, in that he was already there when time began and in that he is the Creator and all the realm of nature is created. God is the Creator; we are created by him. God is the Sustainer; we are sustained by him.

The Bible indicates that God, who is primary, has revealed himself to human beings, who are dependent on that which is primary, both in nature and in the Bible. The former is often referred to as the natural revelation. As stated in Psalm 19:1, "The heavens are telling of the glory of God, and the firmament is showing the work of His hands." Thus, for anyone to make observations in the realm of nature ("the heavens … and the firmament"), he or she is actually observing something of "the glory of God" and "the work of His hands." To be sure, such an observer may or may not have conscious realization or awareness of God's primary role in it. That the Bible is God's written or special revelation of himself to man has been referred to earlier in this book.

We noted in chapter one that context is one of the important factors in the interpretation of specific statements in the Bible. Since both the Bible and nature are means by which God has revealed himself to humankind, nature may legitimately be taken as part of the total context for the interpretation of biblical statements, and vice versa. This, then, is why we said in chapter one that both the Bible and the scientific investigation of nature were being taken as valid sources of information, and why we have tried to include information coming from both sources in subsequent chapters.

In summary, then, Christianity is a total world view based on the God of the Bible as the primary fact: God has revealed himself to human beings both in nature which he created and in the Bible of which he is the ultimate author. Scientism and biblicism are narrower, more restricted world views in which only one, either scientific knowledge or biblical knowledge respectively, is accepted as valid.

Presuppositions and Paradigms

By presupposition, we mean a piece of information, a principle, or an attitude that a person accepts as valid and correct, without personally deriving or proving it, as one draws conclusions and does further work. There indeed are presuppositions in scientific work, and also in biblical interpretation and theology. A full discussion of this topic is beyond the scope of the present book, but some brief comments are appropriate here.

It is convenient to classify presuppositions into two categories, both of which are applicable to uses of the Bible and scientific investigation of nature as sources of information. First, there are many practical presuppositions that the practitioner either in science or in biblical interpretation inevitably encounters in his or her day-by-day work. In science this category includes such detailed items as the labels on bottles of chemicals, the scale markings on indicating meters, and the reference data tabulated in various handbooks and reference sources. It would be impossible for any worker in science "to start from scratch" and to take the time to verify personally that every label is correct, that every indicating meter is calibrated accurately, and that all the reference data are valid. Nevertheless, the scientist is — or at least should be — fully aware of these matters and frequently does take steps to verify them. In biblical theology and interpretation, this category of presupposition often includes the assumption that the biblical text with which one works is a reasonably accurate equivalent of the original writings, the canonicity of the accepted books (and of the rejected ones as well) has been decided correctly, word-studies prepared by language specialists are reasonably accurate, and some summary statements and even detailed explanations provided in scholarly commentaries have some significant degree of validity. It would surely be impossible for any one biblical interpreter or theologian to take the time, even if possessing the required expertise, to verify personally all items of these sorts. Again, however, one should be fully aware of such factors and, when appropriate and feasible, may check them carefully to verify their validity.

The second category of presuppositions includes those that are more basic and thus which are fundamental to the very structure of science or of biblical theology. We may list three of the most basic presuppositions of science as follows.

a. Nature (that is, the physical realm) is real. This presupposition has occasionally been questioned by philosophers, and there is impreciseness in this short statement about just how much and what is assumed to be real. But scientists normally accept it readily as so obvious that it hardly merits a thought. Einstein is quoted as stating, "The belief in an external world independent of the perceiving subject is the basis of all the natural sciences."

b. Nature is orderly, or rational, in that it is consistent and uniform in total cause-effect relationships. This is a very broad and significant principle which, having arisen out of the development of science, has really become an article of faith for scientists. It includes the faith that a particular series of events always results in a unique effect and a given effect in nature is produced not capriciously but from some definable cause or combination of causes. Without this presupposition of the orderliness of nature, there could be no science as it exists today.

c. Nature is, in part, understandable. This is a twofold presupposition, both parts of which are tremendously significant. A longing to know and to understand underlies scientific work. Yet, one's full confidence in the understandability of nature is tempered and also challenged onward by the recognition that scientific knowledge of nature is never absolutely complete or perfect.

In biblical studies this second category of presuppositions, those which are quite basic to the very structure of the body of knowledge which is biblical theology, includes three which are analogous to those listed above for science.

a. The God of the Bible is real. People in various times throughout recorded history have attempted to prove or to disprove that God exists. Yet the Bible itself seems to assume that God exists without attempting to prove it, or, for that matter, even to consider any possibility that the assumption is not correct. As we have already noted, the Bible begins in Genesis 1:1 with a declaration of his existence, "In the beginning God …" and then proceeds in the same verse to state something that he did. In Hebrews 11:6, it is specifically stated that God's existence is something to be accepted by belief, "… for he who comes to God must believe that He is." Furthermore, the Bible designates the person who does not accept God's existence as a presupposition to be a fool, Psalm 14:1, "The fool has said in his heart, 'There is no God.'"

b.	The God of the Bible is orderly, or rational, in the sense that he is consistent and not self-contradictory. This is not to say that God's actions every day are identical with those of every other day, nor even that God treats everyone the same, regardless of individual circumstances and conditions. It would be just as preposterous to say that if there is consistency in the realm of nature, then it must rain every day if it rains one day, or all people are six feet tall if some people are six feet tall. Rather, this presupposition is to say that the God of the Bible is unchanging in his essential being. This principle is stated, for example, in Hebrews 13:8 as, "Jesus Christ is the same yesterday and today, yes and forever." This principle is very basic to the total world view of Christianity, in which it is the same God who underlies and permeates all of nature and the Bible.

c.	The God of the Bible is, in part, understandable. One part of this presupposition, that God is understandable and knowable, is indicated for example in 1 John 5:13, "These things I have written to you who believe in the name of the Son of God, *in order that you may know* that you have eternal life" and in Ezekiel 6:7, "And the slain will fall among you, and *you will know that I am the Lord*" (italics added). The other part of this presupposition, that this understanding is only partial and not complete or perfect, is illustrated by the statements in Isaiah 55:8-9, "For my thoughts are not your thoughts, neither are your ways my ways, declares the Lord. For as the heavens are higher than the earth, so are my ways higher than your ways, and my thoughts than your thoughts," and in 1 Corinthians 13:9, 12, "For we know in part, and we prophecy in part. For now we see in a mirror dimly, but then face to face; now I know in part, but then I shall know fully just as I also have been fully known." Were it not for the presupposition that God is understandable, it would be meaningless to seek to interpret the Bible in terms of God and his actions. Were it not for the presupposition that human beings, at least in this life, do not achieve perfect and complete understanding and knowledge of God, much of biblical content and instruction would be meaningless or even contradictory.

A study of the historical development of scientific knowledge and of its presuppositions in both categories leads one to the conclusion that consideration is given to dropping a presupposition whenever (1) it is not useful and meaningful, which is to say, if it is not subject to test and thus used for something other than itself, and/or (2) it leads to unreasonable difficulties, especially if some proposed alternative leads to less difficulty or even to different difficulty.

These same two factors are applicable to considerations of dropping presuppositions of biblical interpretation and theology as well. The first is illustrated, for example, by the concept of the "God-of-the-gaps," which has been popular in some eras and in some cultures, as a concept useful in "explaining" natural phenomena for which rational scientific explanations were not known. As scientific understandings develop, such gaps seemingly diminish in size and in number so that the presupposition of this kind of god could be discarded as no longer useful. It should be emphasized here, however, that a "God of the gaps" is not the God of the Bible.

The second factor, the discarding of a presupposition if it leads to unreasonable difficulties, is illustrated in the testimonies of people who conclude that God is not real because they do not find the practical evidences of God's existence or character as they assume it to be or as they wish it were. Consider, for example, the cosmonaut who is reported to have said in effect that there is no God because he did not see him during a space flight, or a person who concludes that God is not real because there is suffering and tragedy in the world. Again, the God of such presuppositions as those is not the God of the Bible. Conversely, there are people who read of the God of the Bible, for example, in Psalm 34:8, "O taste and see that the Lord is good; How blessed is the man who takes refuge in Him!" and who testify from their own experience that this God is real.

The practical significance of presuppositions in any field of learning and knowledge may be described further by reference to what are sometimes called paradigms. The term paradigm here refers to the total complex of a field of learning or of some area within that field. It includes the concepts which are generally accepted as true within that field, along with its languages, theories, and methodologies. It determines to a considerable extent the way in which a person involved in that field sees the data and receives other input information, the experiments undertaken and the things to look for as one seeks to expand or improve the knowledge and understanding, and the interpretations to impart to the input information. A person's paradigms govern his or her mind-set within any field of learning.

People are generally reluctant to discard to any significant degree the paradigms of their fields. Within science this is illustrated by the reluctance of Joseph Priestley (1733-1804) to discard his personal adherence to the alchemical phlogiston theory of combustion, although it was his own discovery of oxygen that enabled others to overthrow that theory. Scientists sometimes miss observations that are discordant with their paradigms simply because they are not looking for them. An example of this was the failure to detect nuclear fission of uranium atoms in certain experiments for some time, because scientists were looking for elements of higher atomic number and thus missed the lighter fission products. What a person "sees," so to speak, is dependent not only on what one is looking at but also on what previous experience has taught one to see.

The situation is surely analogous in biblical interpretation and biblical theology. Paradigms do exist, and people are very reluctant to discard their paradigms to any significant degree, even when other people concurrently hold to differing or contradictory mind-sets. Two people, one schooled in the Bible as a believer in God's ultimate authorship and another schooled in a purely humanistic vein in which the Bible is considered simply ancient human literature, can approach the study of the Bible and see different things in it, both becoming more confirmed in their paradigms. On a somewhat different scale, and at the risk of oversimplification, two people convinced of different doctrinal distinctives can see support for their own viewpoints as they study and interpret the Bible, with little or no valid support for each other's views. For example, a liberal theologian and an evangelical theologian may look for, and "see," different things in the Bible as both of them interpret it based on their own paradigms.

Paradigms are of extreme significance in dealing with the overall subject matter of this book. A well-known historical example, which is not at all controversial today, may provide some perspective for considering more current situations. The conflict between Galileo (1564-1642) and the hierarchy of the church of which he was a member took place at a time when there was a dominant view that the earth was the center of the solar system and that the sun revolved about the earth. This conflict began as one of opposing scientific paradigms. However, it quickly expanded to one involving church leadership because the earth-centered view was considered supported by the Bible, for example, in Psalm 93:1, "The Lord reigns, He is clothed with majesty; the Lord has clothed and girded Himself with strength; indeed *the world is firmly established, it will not be moved"* (italics added). Galileo's support of the then-new scientific view that the sun was the center of the solar system and that the earth rotated around the sun, rather than vice versa, was vigorously opposed. How could the earth move in orbit around the sun, it was asked, if indeed the Bible included Psalm 93:1? In retrospect now, it can safely be said that the anti-Galileo view was based on the prevailing paradigms or mind-sets of the times in both science and theology rather than on a legitimate interpretation of the scientific record and biblical content.

Several recent generations of people have been led to assume, in many instances as parts of their paradigms, that the Bible and modern science are mutually contradictory in the interpretations of their respective sources of information concerning origins. For example, it has widely been assumed in some eras that the Bible teaches that the earth was initially formed about six thousand years ago. Accordingly many Bible believers not only refused to accept, but openly and vigorously opposed, scientific evidences that the earth is much older than that. Even now, at a time when most Bible believers reject that particular interpretation of what the Bible does say on this topic, new generations of people, who do not particularly attribute any validity to the Bible, ridicule it because of what they mistakenly assume that it teaches on this subject.

As another very significant example, several generations of people on both sides of the question have adhered to their paradigms that evolution and creation are inherently contradictory and to unrealistically simplistic versions of what the two terms mean. One consequence is that ridicule is often heaped by zealous adherents of both sides of this conflict on each other, which in turn has the consequence that other people reject the Bible in the name of science, or reject evolution in particular and science or scientists in general in the name of the Bible. It is, of course, impossible for any human being to approach consideration of any topic with a totally open, blank mind. All of us, including me, are influenced by what we already know and think we know and have experienced. To avoid all presuppositions and paradigms is surely as undesirable as it is impossible. However, it is important in the gaining of knowledge and understanding that one make some effort to identify what one's paradigms are and the basis on which they have been derived. To the extent that this is not done, there are tendencies to perpetuate prejudices and biases, misunderstandings, and involvements in building up "straw men" to oppose.

When Problems Arise, ...

The title of this chapter is not intended to imply that no problems are encountered in the joining together of knowledge obtained from the study of the Bible and that derived from the scientific investigation of nature. Indeed, there are such problems and difficulties. Furthermore, there surely are problems which are encountered strictly within the scientific study of nature in fitting one piece of scientific evidence with another. And there surely are problems within the study of the Bible in fitting together different parts of the evidences which it contains. Much of the excitement and motivational enthusiasm of scientific work, and work in biblical theology, is to be found in identifying such problems and in the challenges which they present for further investigation.

Let us consider the topic of what to do when problems arise, whether within science or within biblical theology or between the two, based on a very simple illustration. Suppose that a man wants to know what time it is. Suppose further that he looks first at his wrist watch, which says 2:00, and then at an electric clock on the wall, which says 4:30. Here is an apparent contradiction, for the time cannot be 2:00 and 4:30 simultaneously. First, he reexamines the evidence by looking again at both timepieces to make sure that he read them correctly, by shaking or winding the watch to make sure that it had not run down, and by checking that the wall clock is "plugged in" and that the electricity is "on." Still finding no explanation of the discrepancy and still wanting to know what time it really is, he next seeks additional evidence. For example, he could ask a friend what time his watch says, call a prescribed telephone number for a time check, listen to broadcasts of the National Institute of Standards and Technology over short-wave radio, or tune into a radio or television news broadcast on which periodic time announcements are given. This generally results in resolution of the apparent contradiction, but a third important step should be mentioned — he suspends his judgment as appropriate. Unless or until the apparent contradiction is resolved, he can freely admit that he simply does not know what time it is. The three steps taken in facing the apparent contradiction are (a) reexamine the evidence, (b) seek additional evidence, and (c) suspend judgment as appropriate.

These same three steps are applicable in facing apparent contradictions and in attempting to resolve problems which arise within science, within biblical theology, and in crossovers between the two. Let us illustrate by means of one example that is not now considered to be controversial within each of these three categories. Consider within science some determinations of the density of nitrogen gas which were performed in the laboratory of Lord Rayleigh in 1894. Several batches of nitrogen were prepared by various appropriate means from several different chemical compounds which contained the element nitrogen, and several other batches from dry, carbon dioxide-free air. Experimental measurements of the densities of these batches of nitrogen revealed that the "chemical nitrogen" was less dense than was the "atmospheric nitrogen." Here was an apparent contradiction. After reexamining the evidence and seeking additional evidence of several kinds, it turned out that the "inert gases" were discovered in the atmosphere — a most noteworthy advance in scientific knowledge.

Consider within the area of biblical study, the accounts recorded in the four gospels of the wording placed on the Cross on which Jesus was crucified: Matthew 27:37, "This is Jesus the King of the Jews"; Mark 15:26, "The King of the Jews"; Luke 23:38, "This is the King of the Jews"; and John 19:19, "Jesus the Nazarene, the King of the Jews." These variations of what the inscription said could be considered to be an apparent contradiction. A reexamination of the evidences, including the writing styles and primary intents of the four human authors, can conceivably lead one to the conclusion that each author recorded only that portion of the actual inscription which was most relevant in the context of that particular gospel and that the full inscription was perhaps a composite of the four, "This is Jesus the Nazarene, the King of the Jews." To be sure, there is a bit of uncertainty in this resolution of the apparent contradiction, but there is no significant difficulty in suspending one's judgment and in accepting whatever slight ambiguity may remain.

Consider as a point of crossover between the study of the Bible and the scientific investigation of nature, the question of the age of the earth. A few generations ago, it was commonly concluded that the Bible indicates that the earth came into existence in about 4000 B.C. Scientific study in the realm of nature led to the conclusion that the earth is much, much older than that. Here was an apparent contradiction. The two major evidences for the six-thousand-year-old earth were the assumption that "day" (*yome*) in Genesis means 24-hour periods and the assumption in the interpretations of various recorded genealogies that every generation is listed. Upon reexamining the evidences within the Bible itself, particularly the language and the context factors, it has been generally realized that both assumptions are probably in error (as actually had been recognized many centuries earlier by at least some Bible interpreters). Upon reexamining the scientific evidences for the age of the earth, and upon amassing further such evidences, it became very clear that the earth surely is much, much older than a mere six thousand years. To be sure there is ambiguity even now in assessing the precise age of the earth, and even about what both the scientific evidences and the biblical evidences really do indicate on this point. However, most people who accept both sources of information as valid find themselves reasonably comfortable in living with the uncertainty and ambiguity which exist even now.

It is of great significance to consider now why there even should be any resolution to problems and to apparent contradictions which arise within and between the two fields of learning. According to the Christian world view, it is the same one God who underlies and permeates all of nature (which he created and sustains) and all of the canonical books of the

Bible (of which he was the ultimate author by unique inspiration). Further, according to this world view, God is rational and orderly and knowable (in part) through examinations of his revelations of himself to humankind in nature and in the Bible. On this basis, it is to be expected that there should be no real contradictions within these revelations and that there must be somehow, somewhere a valid resolution of each apparent contradiction which may arise. Indeed, the fact that most apparent contradictions which have arisen have been resolved, through the three-step approach described above, supports the Christian world view but does not, of course, really prove it.

A final point is worthy of emphasis here, that of withholding judgment as appropriate. As far as biblical study is concerned, the Bible itself points out that God is not providing totally the knowledge and understanding which he himself possesses, as we noted on page 100. As far as scientific study of nature is concerned, scientific explanation is never to be considered perfect and complete, as we noted on page 17. Therefore, it is inevitable that there be a degree of ambiguity and uncertainty in human knowledge, whether based on one or the other or both of our two sources of information. There are many points on which we must suspend final judgment, even throughout human life. At the same time, we should recognize that although science and biblical theology cannot provide explanations which are perfect and complete, it does not mean that they cannot provide explanations which have considerable meaning and validity.

Faith and/or Intellect

Within the world view of Christianity, we have been considering the fitting together of information obtained from the Bible and from the scientific study of nature regarding how God does some of the things that he does. In so doing we inevitably encounter the concepts of faith and intellect. There is sometimes a tendency to assume that these two are opposed to each other; and that for a person to exercise faith is to neglect the intellect, or vice versa. However, it is the view of many people, including me, that both are essential within the Christian world view. It is a matter of faith *and* intellect, not faith *or* intellect. Let us illustrate the relationship between the two by considering briefly how people derive their concepts of the existence and nature of God.

Belief in the existence of some kind of supreme being is a characteristic of human beings in all times and in all cultures. The question of who or what that god is or gods are, varies tremendously from time to time, from culture to culture, and from person to person within any particular time and culture. How do people get their concepts of God? One common way is by means of human reasoning.

People as rational, intellectual beings have sought for many centuries to prove by reasoning, at least to their own satisfaction, that some sort of a supreme being exists. Out of these efforts has come a series of classical "proofs," or philosophical arguments, for the existence of God. Some of these depend in part on evidences observable in the realm of nature.

One line of reasoning is the *cosmological argument*, which is based on cause-and-effect relationships. According to this line of reasoning, wherever there is motion, as there is throughout the universe, there must be a source or cause of this motion. Ultimately there must have been a first cause which itself had no source or cause, and this first cause or "prime mover" is (or was) God. Or to state it differently, nothing can be the cause of itself or it would be prior to itself; therefore, there must have been a first cause. A somewhat similar type of reasoning has been applied to concepts of perfection and intelligence. Degrees of perfection are found in the universe; so there must be an ultimate of perfection, which is the supreme being. Or, everything is more or less good, so there must be a "most good," which is the supreme being. Or, there are degrees of intelligence among people, so there must be — in principle at least — an infinite intelligence which is God.

Another philosophical "proof" for the existence of God is the *teleological argument*, which is based on design and purpose in the universe. This one is perhaps the best known and the most compelling of the classical "proofs." It is common among many lay people, who are unfamiliar with any philosophical statements or treatments of it, as well as among some philosophical scholars. There is evidence of apparent design throughout the realm of nature, so it is reasoned that there must be a directing intelligence, which is taken to be the supreme being. Even the evolutionary concepts of the origins and developments of the many forms of life represent a continual striving toward higher forms, so again it is reasoned that there must be a directing intelligence.

A third philosophical line of reasoning is the *ontological argument* for the existence of God, which is a bit more difficult to describe but has received considerable attention over the years. This line of reasoning is not based on any observations in the world, as are the teleological and cosmological arguments. It is in effect an extrapolation from the fact that man has an idea concerning God to the conclusion that God must exist. The very idea of a supreme being implies the existence of such a being. Even the fool who says there is no God (Psalm 14:1) has an idea of God, or else he would not be inclined to deny his existence. Human beings are unique among other living creatures in realizing that there are limits to their own being, and by this realization are really transcending their own being and reaching toward an awareness of potential infinity, toward an awareness of an ultimate. Now, according to the ontological line of reasoning, if one's idea of the ultimate were itself the ultimate, there would not really be an ultimate. So that which is ultimate and infinite must exist apart from any person. Thus, the very idea of the existence of a supreme being points toward the conclusion that a supreme being must exist.

Many rational and intelligent people consider these types of rational arguments for the existence of God to be very persuasive. Many other equally rational and intelligent people come to very different conclusions from the same lines of human reasoning.

Another common means by which people get their concepts of God is based on human experience. One form of human experience is through observations in the realm of nature. The teleological argument described above is one form of this type of claim. It is suggested that no person can study the skies, or the intricacies of atomic and molecular structure, or the wonders of the human eye, as examples, and not believe that there is a God. These suggestions are surely very meaningful, and they are quite compelling as proofs of God to many people. However, there are other people who observe the same phenomena in nature and are equally intelligent and sincere in their interpretations of what they observe, who come to different conclusions with respect to whether there is or is not a supreme being.

Another form of the use of human experience as the basis of a person's concept of God centers on the emotional experiences of human beings. Many people testify about having had personal encounters and experiences with God, and thus to have proved that he exists and that he has particular interrelationships with them. However, alternative explanations of the same experiences are conceivable, in which they are described not as real encounters with a real God, but rather as emotional and "feeling" experiences with psychological rather than theological origins.

Both the rational and the experiential bases for obtaining one's concept of God have in common the facts that they are very meaningful and persuasive to some people but that nontheistic alternative explanations are more acceptable to other people. It appears, then, that faith and belief are essential to any person's concept of God. The philosophical and experiential considerations thus are not proofs in any generally compelling sense for either a theistic or nontheistic basic view, but are interpretable as giving support to whichever basic view one accepts by faith.

It is interesting to note that it is likewise in essence an act of faith and not one of rational or experiential verification for any person to conclude the nonexistence of God. By way of illustration, consider the story of a blatant, self-avowed atheist who was asked, "Just how can you be so absolutely certain that there is no God?" To this the professed atheist responded, "This is simply one of those things that one must accept by faith."

The Bible itself does not undertake to convince its readers of the existence of God by reasoning of human experience. As we noted earlier, it assumes that God exists. It does not even consider in any direct way any possibility that he may not. The Bible refers to objects and events in the realm of nature as testifying to the being and nature of God, but not as inescapable proofs to those who do not believe in faith that he is. The Bible refers to certain human experiences as encounters with God, for example in 1 Corinthians 2. To the person with faith in the God of the Bible, these ongoing experiences with God are very real and meaningful, and provide powerful evidences in support of that faith. However, as 1 Corinthians 2 also points out, the person without this faith simply does not understand the situation in that way.

This discussion, centering on how people get their concepts of the existence and nature of God, can serve to illustrate in a more general way the relationships between faith and the intellect. Both faith and reason are important. Each supplements the other and neither replaces the other.

The term faith is, like so many other common words, difficult to define with precision. It is surely not synonymous with a blind guess, wishful thinking, persistent optimism, positive thinking, mere feeling, or with a desire to escape from present conditions, nor merely something to exercise when other knowledge is lacking. Faith incorporates both the reasoning and the emotional aspects of a person's being. Faith is belief with confidence and trust, as is indicated in Hebrews 1:11, "Now faith is the assurance of things hoped for, the conviction of things not seen." Faith is not contrary to the evidences. It is based on evidences and goes beyond evidences.

In summary, faith and intellect are both essential in the Christian world view. Both are involved in interpreting and understanding both nature and the Bible. It is not merely that one takes over where the other leaves off, but that faith and intellect are closely interrelated and mutually interdependent.

How Big Is God?

The purpose of this section is not to answer the question, "How big is God?" It is to suggest that we tend to limit God unduly in our thinking and understanding of him and his revealed involvements in the realm of nature and the Bible.

In the Christian world view, the God of the Bible is the primary fact. He is the Creator; the universe, the world, life, and humankind are all created. God is the Sustainer of the realm of nature which he has created. He is transcendent to this realm, and is immanent within it. God has revealed himself to humans through that which he created (natural revelation) and through the writings which comprise the Bible (special revelation).

To use the concept of God only to account for and thus to explain phenomena for which no natural explanation is known is to limit God unduly. He is the Originator and the Sustainer of natural laws which we discover and use to describe actions and reactions in the realm of nature.

To limit one's confident knowledge to that obtained from the scientific investigation of nature alone, or from the Bible alone, is to limit God unduly. The same God is responsible for both.

To fear science, or even to reject it, in the name of the Bible is to limit God unduly. The realm of nature shows forth the glory of God to those who by faith believe that he is.

To deny the Bible, or to put it aside as irrelevant, in the name of science is to limit God unduly. The God who created nature is the same God who uniquely inspired the biblical writers.

To fear, or to oppose by ridicule, concepts of origins by processes describable by natural mechanisms is to limit God unduly. For one to know that God was the originator does not necessarily require that he did or did not use any particular mechanisms of his own choosing and his own making.

To assume that naturalistic explanation of any phenomenon rules out the idea that God is in it is to limit God unduly. For natural law is, in essence, a descriptive explanation of what God built into the realm of nature, to which he is transcendent and in which he is immanent.

To limit one's perception of any human being to nothing more than a physical and biological creature, or to a purely intellectual being, is not only to attempt the impossible but is also to limit God. Humankind is unique in all of creation, made in the image of God.

The more one becomes familiar with the realm of nature, recognizing it as the handiwork of God, the more one knows and understands how big God is. The more one becomes familiar with the content of the Bible, recognizing it as the written Word of God, the more one knows and understands how big God is — so big, in fact, that he can know and provide for the individual human being, including you and me, in justice and in love.

Suggestions for Additional Reading

General Works

Berry, R. J., ed. *Real Science, Real Faith*. London: Christian Impact, 1995.

Bube, Richard H. *Putting It All Together: Seven Patterns for Relating Science and the Christian Faith*. Lanham, MD: University Press of America, 1995.

Giberson, Karl. *Worlds Apart: The Unholy War between Religion and Science*. Kansas City, MO: Beacon Hill Press, 1993.

Holder, R. D. *Nothing But Atoms and Molecules? Probing the Limits of Science*. Crowborough, UK: Monarch, 1993.

Hummel, Charles E. *The Galileo Connection: Resolving Conflicts between Science & the Bible*. Downers Grove, IL: InterVarsity Press, 1986.

Lucas, E. *Genesis Today*. London: Christian Impact, 1995.

Polkinghorne, John. *The Faith of a Physicist: Reflections of a Bottom-Up Thinker*. Princeton, NJ: Princeton University Press, 1994.

Polkinghorne, John. *Quarks, Chaos and Christianity: Questions to Science and Religion*. New York: The Crossroad Publishing Company, 1996.

Ratzsch, Del. *The Battle of Beginnings, Why Neither Side is Winning the Creation-Evolution Debate*. Downers Grove, IL: InterVarsity Press, 1996.

Ross, Hugh. *Creation and Time: A Biblical and Scientific Perspective on the Creation-Date Controversy*. Colorado Springs, CO: NavPress, 1994.

Wilkinson, D. A. *God, The Big Bang and Stephen Hawking*. Crowborough, UK: Monarch, 1993.

Young, Davis A. *The Biblical Flood: A Case Study of the Church's Response to Extrabiblical Evidence*. Grand Rapids, MI: William B. Eerdmans Publishing Co., 1995.

Specialized Works

Committee for Integrity in Science Education. *Teaching Science in a Climate of Controversy*, fourth printing. Ipswich, MA: American Scientific Affiliation, 1993.

Haas, Jr., J. W., ed. *Perspectives on Science and Christian Faith.* Journal of the American Scientific Affiliation. Ipswich, MA: American Scientific Affiliation.

Kaiser, Christopher. *Creation and the History of Science.* Grand Rapids, MI: William B. Eerdmans Publishing Co., 1991.

Johnson, Philip. *Reasons in the Balance: The Case Against Naturalism in Science, Law and Education.* Downers Grove, IL: InterVarsity Press, 1995.

Moreland, J. P. *Christianity and the Nature of Science: A Philosophical Investigation.* Grand Rapids, MI: Baker Book House, 1989.

Numbers, Ronald L. *The Creationists, The Evolution of Scientific Creationism.* New York: Alfred A. Knopf, Inc., 1992.

Index

A

Abraham, 27, 35, 44
Age of the earth, 51-53, 107
Agnostic, 6, 39, 50, 68
   definition, 38
Amalekites, 28-29
Anatomy
   comparative, 59
Apollos, 34
Asah, 47
Assyrians, 29-30, 39
Astrology, 86
Atheism, 6, 33, 39
Augustine, 45

B

Bara, 46-47
Bible, 9-14, 20-21, 23-24, 42,
   63, 112
   See also New Testament
   See also Old Testament
Biblical
   See also inspiration
   interpretation, 10-12, 97-98,
   101-102
   theology, 93-94, 97-101
Biblicism, 92, 97
   definition, 95
Big bang model, 55
Biochemistry, 59

C

Canon, 9, 93, 98, 107

Cause-and-effect relationships,
   5-7, 16, 54, 86-87, 109
Chance, 70
Chemical reagents, 57
Christian church, 33, 35, 75, 77
Christianity, 92, 95-97, 107-
   109, 113
   definition, 96
Confidence levels, 15-19, 60-61
Copernican view, 55
Cosmological argument, 109
Cosmology, 54
   definition, 53
Creation, 67-70
Creator, 3, 40, 45-46, 48, 84,
   96, 113

D

Daniel, 76
Day, 44-46, 63-65, 107
Day of Pentecost, 33
Deism, 3
Dunamis, 73

E

Earth
   old, 43-45, 104, 107
   young, 43-45, 104, 107
Egypt, 27-28, 73, 75-76, 78
Einstein, 16, 98
Elijah, 75-76
Elisha, 75-76
Elkanah, 35

M

Magic, 86
Mary, 77
Materialism
definition, 92
Midianites, 28-29
Milky Way, 55
Miracle, 72-83
at Cana, 82
definition, 74
Model
See also big bang model
definition, 16
scientific, 16-17, 94
Mopheth, 72-73
Moses, 75-77, 81
Mutations, 57

N

Natural, 83-85, 87
means, 5, 7, 28-30, 36, 40
mechanisms, 5-7, 38-39, 46-48, 80
processes, 32, 36-38, 46
revelation, 96, 113
selection, 57-58
theology, 93
Naturalism, 91
Nature, 8, 22, 97-99
definition, 4, 83, 93
study, 20-21
New Testament, 9-10, 21, 23, 33, 93
See also Bible

O

Old Testament, 9-10, 21, 23,
27, 33, 93
See also Bible
Ontological argument, 110
Origen, 45
Origins, 66, 68
how, 45-48, 53, 64-65
See also human reproduction
when, 43, 51-53, 63-64
who, 42, 50
Owth, 72-73

P

Pala, 72-73
Pantheism, 3
Paradigm, 97, 102-104
definition, 102
Paul, 3, 34, 73
Philip, 34, 73
Physical
causes, 39
universe, 54
Physiology
comparative, 59
Presupposition, 97-102, 104
definition, 97
Presuppositions, 15-16

Q

Quantum mechanics, 55

R

Radioactive decay, 51-52
Rationalism
definition, 92
Red Sea, 76, 78, 80, 83

Organizations Focusing on Science/Faith Issues

About the ASA

Founded in 1941, the American Scientific Affiliation (ASA) is a fellowship of over 2,000 Christians in the sciences committed to understanding the relationship of science to the Christian faith. The stated purposes of the ASA are "to investigate any area relating Christian faith and science" and "to make known the results of such investigations for comment and criticism by the Christian community and by the scientific community." For more information, contact ASA, P. O. Box 668, Ipswich, MA 01938-0668.

About the CiS

Christians in Science (CiS — formerly the Research Scientist's Christian Fellowship) was founded in 1942 in the United Kingdom. Among its 750 members are scientists, philosophers, theologians, ministers, and others with an interest in science-religion questions. It seeks to promote a positive Christian view of the nature, scope, and limitations of science in the modern world, to develop clearly thought out Christian views of the changing interactions between science and faith, to encourage Christians who are involved with science to maintain a lively faith and apply it to their discipline, and to present a Christian viewpoint in the world of science and the wider community. For more information, contact Mrs. Pauline Williams, Membership Secretary, 102 Midhurst Road, Kings Norton, Birmingham B30 3RD ENGLAND.